CW00644334

From the Lines of Dissent

First Edition

Copyright © Out-Spoken Press 2016
Copyright © Media Diversified 2016

First published in 2016 by
Out-Spoken Press & Media Diversified

Design & Art Direction
Ben Lee

Printed & Bound by:
Print Resources

Typeset in: Px Grotesk

ISBN: 978-0-9931038-8-9

From the Lines
of Dissent

Essays on race, religion & identity
by people of colour.

OUT
SPOKEN
PRESS.

MEDIA
DIVERSIFIED
M/D

Contents

Foreword

Gary Younge

WHEN asked whether she found the description of "black woman writer" limiting Toni Morrison replied : "I'm already discredited. I'm already politicised, before I get out of the gate. I can accept the labels because being a black woman writer is not a shallow place but a rich place to write from. It doesn't limit my imagination, it expands it."

It is that tone of defiance, that awareness of framing and that embrace of myriad identities that makes this collection of articles from Media Diversified both so engaging and important. There is a sharp intelligence here and some crisp critiques. But it is the fearlessness to take on the dominant narratives – of race among others - in ways that are both playful and polemic that are most striking.

To define oneself, ones priorities, desires, needs and enemies, is philosophically one of the most potent weapons we have. It not only gives us voice – that indispensable tool of all journalism - it gives us form, purpose and authority. Without self-definition whatever meaning we derive from the world must first be refracted through the ego of another, more powerful less qualified entity. "If I didn't define myself for myself," said the late journalist and writer Audre Lorde, " I would be crunched into other people's fantasies for me and eaten alive."

What is most inspiring about the work here is that it starts from the point and principal of self-definition. The writers do not accept words they don't respect and do not respect terminology that doesn't honour them. Instead they seek to create a new premise which does not seek to include them as an afterthought but in which their experiences are integral from the outset. This is heavy-lifting. But it is worth it.

Why black people need this ought to be self-evident in a moment we are literally fighting to assert our humanity against violent states, hostile media and exclusory borders. What has sadly been less obvious to some is why white people need it to. But it is becoming increasingly evident that the partial, privileged understanding of how this world works and where they stand in it is not serving them well. Whether its Brexit in Britain or the nomination of Donald Trump in America, the lack of non-white voices and anti-racist critiques has helped degrade entire political cultures with far-reaching consequences.

"Our opinions cover a bigger space, a longer reach of time, a greater number of things, than we can directly observe," wrote Walter Lippmann in his landmark book, Public Opinion. "They have, therefore, to be pieced together out of what others have reported."

But what others have reported is insufficient. Those inadequacies will not correct themselves. They need organisations to challenge them and individuals to reframe them. That is what Media Diversified does; that is what these pieces do.

Decolonise, not Diversify

Kavita Bhanot

The successive failures of initiatives like World Book Night and literary prizes to include writers of colour in their lists has precipitated a fresh bout of conversation about the need for more 'diversity' in the literature that is published and awarded in Britain, as well as amongst those working in publishing.

Alongside a series of Guardian articles, there was a call for contributions to Nikesh Shukla's crowd-funded anthology on race and immigration (in itself a great idea); writers of colour were invited to come forward, to contact Shukla. #diversedecember, a twitter initiative set up by bloggers Naomi Frisby and Dan Lipscombe, that encouraged people to 'read with diversity' and share the 'diverse' books that they are reading. Many organisations and individuals, readers and writers, joined in to help bring more 'diversity' to publishing.

To whom is all this directed? Who should read more 'diverse' literature? For whom is literature written by minority writers 'diverse'? For whom are minority writers 'diverse'? Can I describe myself as 'diverse' – do I exist in that space called 'diversity'?

The concept of diversity only exists if there is an assumed neutral point from which 'others' are 'diverse.' Putting aside for now the straight, male, middle-classness of that 'neutral' space, its dominant aspect is whiteness. Constructed by a white establishment, the idea of 'diversity' is neo-liberal speak. It is the new corporatized version of multiculturalism. It is about management, efficiency, box-ticking. As writers of colour, we parrot this idea back, reminding white institutions that they need to increase their diversity; appealing to them to let us in, to give some of us a seat at the table too. To help convince them, institutions are reminded that 'diversity' is actually good for them too, that it will help them to make more money. Danuta Keane writes, in the 'Writing the Future' report on the need for improved cultural/ethnic diversity in literature:

'this isn't about making the industry feel good. Mono-cultures are bad for business....within 20 years the UK BAME population will be 25%. If books don't reflect that, they will become increasingly irrelevant and unprofitable.' Similarly, Shukla writes in a Guardian article: 'I wouldn't be wasting my time if I didn't feel there was a potential financial reward for investing in BAME writers.' Meanwhile, a tweet on #diversedecember tells us, through a posted article, that 'just being around people of different ethnicities may literally make you smarter.'

Although the lack of interest in our work on the part of white publishers is a very real problem, when we respond to and celebrate 'diversity', we don't deeply challenge a white system. We only appeal to it, try to fit ourselves into it, make ourselves attractive to it to, trying to sell our 'diversity'. We go to workshops that tell us how, as BAME writers, we can brand ourselves better, package ourselves, make ourselves more marketable; to get funding, to find a publisher, to sell books. And in this way, we define ourselves through this system, softening ourselves, performing our identities and ethnicities for it. Perhaps there's little choice when you're entering the mainstream space as an isolated individual, as a writer or an editor; it's the only way to get in and survive. We don't talk about racism, just 'lack of diversity'. As Ellen Berry says in her article, 'Diversity is for white people: The big lie behind a well-intended word', 'Diversity is how we talk about race when we can't talk about race. It has become a stand-in when open discussion of race is too controversial or — let's be frank — when white people find the topic of race uncomfortable. Diversity seems polite, positive, hopeful.'

And it's just this non-threatening positivity, hopefulness and cheery celebration that we've seen in this new phase of 'diversity in literature' campaigning, co-curated by the Guardian, drawing on data and recommendations by the recent 'Spread the Word' report. '#diversedecember is a celebration of books by BAME writers. For December 2015, read with diversity and spread the joy of stories' is the message on the twitter page for this worthy cause. 'Diverse December lifts the Christmas spirits,' writes Jackie Kay in the double-page article in Guardian Review, 'How do we stop UK publishing being so posh and white?' Meanwhile, the extraordinary success of Nikesh Shukla's crowd-funded anthology of essays about race and immigration has left him feeling 'a mixture of relief and vindication that there is such a fierce appetite for BAME voices out there.' Such diversity campaigns make it all look so easy.

Through one concrete action, or perhaps a list of actions, everyone can help to sort out the problem. You can recommend your favourite 'diverse' book on #diversedecember. Feeling virtuous, you can read a 'diverse' book this month; a bit like medicine, reading a diverse book is good for you, it opens up your mind, teaches you about another culture/country. 'Today, we'd really like to receive recommendations of books by Muslim authors, please!' #diversedecember tweeted on the 9th December 2015. 'Also don't neglect your genre fiction in #diversedecember – crime novels especially are an amazing way of reading about non-Western life,' says one retweet.

Or you can contribute money to the proposed collection of essays on 'race and immigration' (avoiding the word 'racism'). 'I think this will be an important, timely read. Help fund The Good Immigrant (I've donated at link below)' tweets JK Rowling. (How can race, racism or immigration be timely, you wonder, 'flavour of the month'?)

Rowling, after a generous contribution, is now patron of Shukla's anthology. Her name will grace the front cover of the book. Nobody questions the fact that a book on 'race and immigration' has also now become about Rowling as celebrity white saviour. 'JK Rowling inspires surge to fund book on race and immigration in three days,' the Guardian article, carrying her photograph, tells us. This is the same writer who was criticised in two excellent letters by Mia Oudeh (a fan of the Harry Potter series), for signing the 'Culture for Coexistence' letter, supporting Israeli-Palestinian dialogue and opposition to the BDS movement. According to Rowling, 'boycotts singling out Israel are divisive and discriminatory'.

Like accusations of reverse racism or casteism, there is not only naïvete, but also violence in erasing historical and continuing oppressions and power hierarchies, labelling the oppressed who seek to redress, 'divisive' and 'discriminatory'. It is the same conciliatory, ahistorical approach that can ground these diversity in literature campaigns. There is a sense that everyone only needs to come together, make a bit of an effort with a few simple acts. Diversity is about forgetting the past, and celebrating a multi-coloured present. Diversity initiatives often involve a Benetton style ad of 'diverse looking' people's faces, and we see such an image adorning the cover of the Guardian Review which contains the aforementioned article, 'How do we stop UK publishing being so posh and white?'

In this article, various writers, publishers, organisers of festivals have listed the things that they have done or pledge to do to improve the situation. Jackie Kay tells us that Carol Ann Duffy has offered to give up her place on the list of books for World Book Night for a 'diverse' writer. Nick Barley, Director of the Edinburgh International Book Festival pledges that he will, among other things, 'buy another copy of The Fishermen by Chigozie Obioma and give it to someone as a Christmas present'; 'try to persuade Chimamanda Ngozi Adichie to visit the UK with a group of emerging African writers'; 'invite Jackie Kay to talk to Syrian refugees in Scotland and share their stories at the book festival" and 'ask Kamila Shamsie and Mohammed Hanif to recommend Pakistani writers not yet known here, and invite them to Edinburgh'. Meanwhile Simon Prosser of Hamish Hamilton writes in the same article, 'luckily, there are partners we can work with. The Caine prize for African writing, the Muslim writers awards and the DSC prize for south Asian literature, for example, do a great job in showcasing diverse writers, as do magazines such as Wasafiri and SABLE LitMag'.

We see here one of the problems with quick-fixes to the 'diversity' problem: they usually involve reaching out for the handful of well-known names, writers, organisations that imm-ediately come to mind, promoting them or asking them for advice and recommendations (although there have been some new and lesser known writers recommended and highlighted on #diversedecember). Not to undermine the good work that some of these magazines and prizes do, but this approach ensures that literature remains in the same circles of power, within one class and caste. Such tokenism also means that it is often the writers of colour who are most visible, who work the hardest to turn themselves into shiny friendly packages, who are most acceptable and amenable, that are reached for. These includes international writers who are westernised, cosmopolitan, upper class and upper caste, or British writers whose ideologies and world views, articulated through their fiction and non-fiction, most resemble that of white Britain, right wing or left-liberal. My research, which has included close readings of contem-porary published British Asian literature, has shown that the writers who overtly spout the kind of racism that it is no longer 'politically correct' for a white public figure to articulate, are often the most visible and celebrated. The racism in the books and articles by these writers is acceptable, since they are of South Asian origin, and it is invisible because it is normalised in British society. It is perhaps inevitable that writers who are a product of British society, education, literature, media, will internalise and reproduce white supremacy. The literature they write is directed towards white readers; it is about Britishness, about assimilation, about becoming a British citizen. Their representations of 'difference' often feed racism and stereotypes, with their focus primarily on the 'reverse racism' of their families and communities.

It is perhaps not an accident that these writers are so often given a voice and platform. Diversity boxes are ticked, without really shaking things up too much. Even within this double-page spread Guardian article, two or three of the writers, doing okay themselves, undermine the claimed intention of the piece by writing that they don't really see that there is too much of a problem. Sarfraz Manzoor 'would be wary of an excessive focus on race and religion', while Akhil Sharma feels that he has actually 'benefited from being an ethnic writer ... Because I am writing about things that are not well known, and I am writing about a community that people are curious about, I have received a great deal of attention ... my complaining would feel churlish since I have benefited so much from being a minority'.

Who are the 'people' who are curious about the community that Sharma is writing about, allowing him to 'benefit' from his ethnicity? Certainly not the community he is writing about. It is clear in what Sharma says, who his work is directed towards, who he writes for. 'People' here equals white people. So much of our writing consciously or unconsciously reproduces this assumption, and subtly reveals internalised white supremacy. There was an uproar when Marlon James talked about the pressure on writers to pander to white women, but such pressures, on the part of agents and editors, are real. Although it is not necessarily a conscious, cynical pandering, we often unconsciously direct our work towards the white reader, privileging the white reader, since that is the normative perspective. We will continue to do this unless we consciously interrogate ourselves, unless we read each others work and our own critically, to 'see' white supremacy (along with upper class and caste, male, heterosexual supremacy) in what has come before and what continues to be produced. In order to write differently. This will certainly not happen in university creative writing courses, mentoring schemes, through mainstream editors or discussions at literature festivals, where white literature is held up as the 'real' literature that we all need to aspire towards.

Adopting a phrase that is being used by radical anti-racist campaigns and movements growing and connecting across the world today, as writers and editors we need to 'de-colonise, not diversify', and that is what we need to demand of publishers, creative writing courses, and mentoring schemes too. Decolonisation does not airbrush colonial history, decolonisation takes continuing white supremacy head-on. And if publishers or organisers of literature festivals are not interested in literature that comes from this place, that doesn't privilege the white reader, we need to use models such as Shukla's crowd-funded book, to produce our own literature. We need to organise our own festivals. There are writers, publishers and organisations that have been and continue, despite all odds, doing this.

But to focus only on numbers, as the 'Writing the Future' report does, to talk only about the need for a greater 'diversity' of writers in terms of background, is a limited and misleading approach. The real problem is not simply a monoculture but a mono-ideology, a mono-perspective. I'm sorry to spoil the party, but this is not a problem that was going to be solved this December or even, now that #diversitydecember has become #ReadDiverse2016.

Kavita Bhanot lives between India and England and is currently teaching at Ashoka University in India. She has a PhD from Manchester University in Creative Writing and Literature. Her fiction and non-fiction has been published widely in anthologies, magazines and journals, two of her stories have been broadcast on BBC Radio 4. She is editor of the anthology Too Asian, Not Asian Enough (Tindal Street Press 2011) and is co-editor with Courttia Newland, of the forthcoming Bare Lit anthology (Brain Mill Press/Media Diversified. She is a reader with The Literary Consultancy

Why Science Fiction Matters to Life in the Postcolony

Haris A. Durrani

I remember learning about the Sykes-Picot Agreement of 1916, that moment when Britain and France drew lines on a map of what is now known as the Middle East. I was in high school in the U.S., and the so-called Arab Spring had just erupted on the other side of the world. The headlines about the uprisings felt as surreal and alive as Europe's border-sketching pen seemed bizarre and artificial. They were as strange as the transformation of Ronald Reagan's freedom-fighting, Commie-crushing Mujahidin into Osama Bin Laden's nefarious Al-Qaeda. My immediate, geek-addled thought to the region's unfolding events? This is something out of science fiction.

In fact, it was. The similarities between what's been happening in the wider Middle East and Frank Herbert's science fiction novel Dune (1965) are striking. In the novel, which celebrates its 50th anniversary this year, aristocratic houses and a futuristic emperor vied for control over the titular planet, the only source of "the spice." The spice, an invaluable substance both drug and interstellar fuel, was Herbert's reference to oil. The planet was inhabited by Fremen, a Bedouin-like people who used their familiarity with the land and its giant sandworms to resist their oppressors. The Fremen could be the Pashtuns or the Mujahidin, or this uprising or that one. The giant, desert-dwelling sandworms evoked the unconquerable landscape of Afghanistan or Iraq or Syria, where chaos still follows after western powers incessantly fail to install new order. The Fremen language was akin to Arabic and their mythology to Islamic mysticism, theology, and eschatology.

Perhaps Herbert was writing about Britain's conquest of Arabia. Or perhaps he was predicting the Hollywood comedy-drama Charlie Wilson's War, or the U.S. invasion of Iraq in 2003. Or, more crudely, the end of days. Like the emperor and barons perched above Dune, Europe and America loomed over its othered territories, unleashing armies, diplomats, and engineers in the surreal project of colonisation.

But Dune is more than a direct allegory for the tragic unfolding of history. It recasts the Middle East and North Africa and its peoples into a new, and perhaps truer, image of themselves; an image that can only be appreciated through the experience of reading. Yes, events have not unfolded as triumphantly as they do for the Fremen. But the literature of science fiction and fantasy expresses the irrationality with which the real world violently comes into being. It draws out the metaphors with which reality is made.

Take Iraqi novelist Hassan Blasim, author of a recently published collection of short stories, The Corpse Exhibition: And Other Stories of Iraq (2014). He meshes the absurd with the real, the dark with the satiric, Borges with Poe, on the canvas of contemporary Iraq. In his short story The Reality and the Record (2011), Blasim narrates the life of a fictional ambulance driver in Baghdad who is kidnapped by a militia group. The man is dressed in a uniform and forced to read a script before a camera. Reading the script, he announces he is an Iraqi army officer who, following U.S. orders, has committed war crimes. The driver plays the part so well that the members of the militia sell him to another group, which then sells him to another, and so on. In each act the driver takes on a new role, pretending to be Sunni or Shi'a Muslim, Kurdish, Christian, Saudi, Baathist, Iranian, Al-Qaeda leadership, and even Spanish. He crosses sides until his newfound career as enslaved actor rises to bleak, satiric fame within the strange subculture of the Iraqi militia propaganda machine. Reputable news outlets, including Al Jazeera, are tricked by the driver's multiple characters, never realising the same man is in every recording. After eighteen months, the driver is let go. He learns only a single night has passed since his capture. No one believes his story, including his own family. He suspects the world has conspired against him. "The world is just a bloody and hypothetical story," one of Blasim's characters scorns, "and we are all killers and heroes." After immigrating to Sweden, the driver is eventually declared insane.

Most of Blasim's stories are like this. Like the stories of the Iraqi post-war author Ahmed Saadawi, whose Frankenstein in Baghdad (2014) won The International Prize for Arabic Fiction in 2014, Blasim's fiction embody figments of his characters' paranoia and trauma. But the tangibility of their most absurd moments are hard to shake. "You can turn the woman who sells fish in the market into a spaceship lost in the cosmos, or turn aubergines into a philosophy lesson," one of his protagonists, a writer, remarks. "The important thing is to observe at length, like someone contemplating suicide from a balcony." Blasim eschews the presumptions of the western gaze and intensifies his characters' suffering in ways that do not exoticise, escape, or divert from their tragedies but display them, oddly, as they truly are. His stories read like perfect slices of modern Iraq, more real than what you might encounter in the pages of The New York Times. For a post-war Iraqi, Blasim suggests, reality is absurd.

I encountered this phenomenon while writing my novella, Technologies of the Self (Brain Mill Press). The book is based in part on my uncle's immigration to the U.S. from the Dominican Republic around the time of the second U.S. occupation in 1965. The story recounts a series of trials he faced upon arrival in New York, mixing actual events from his life with time travel and demons. I leave the reader – and myself, at times – unsure of what is or isn't real. Perusing early drafts, my peers remarked that my demonic time-travelling conquistador "space knight" felt real. A gang in a Washington Heights alleyway stabbing my uncle in the chest with a pickaxe for pocket change did not. To them, the parts I knew to be true were too nonsensical or absurd to be believable. Technologies of the Self is ultimately a work of fiction. But I hope that doesn't make it any less true.

The history and politics of the MENA, other postcolonial regions, and the diasporas which I am a part of feel closer to science fiction than science fiction itself. The development of modernity and the state are ambiguous and elusory as much as they are bizarre and artificial, like Sykes-Picot or Herbert's ominous emperor. They forgo an empirical analysis. Likewise, resistance to colonialism's lasting and discursive forms of power lives equally beyond the boundaries of academic definition.

People are much the same. To tell things as they are, their stories must often tell them as they are not. Stories, then, are our means of digging beneath both polemics and 'the facts on the ground'. They are a vessel toward the deepest kind of understanding. This is what the Muslim theologian, jurist, and philosopher Al-Ghazali called dhawq, or fruitional experience. That concept is embedded in the heart of science fiction and fantasy literature.

This is why science fiction and fantasy is such a powerful tool for the postcolonial life. In its simplest form, the genre can provide escapism, a haven from the ongoing daily strife. Meanwhile, dystopias usefully warn us how to navigate or avoid oppressive regimes. And in its most potent form, science fiction and fantasy literature sheds light on the complex architecture of the real world. It helps writers and their readers break out of binaries of oppression and marginal-isation, transcend stereotypes, and imagine new ways of living.

Haris A. Durrani is an author, engineer, and academic. His debut, Technologies of the Self, won the Driftless Novella Contest (Brain Mill Press). He is a J.D. candidate at Columbia Law School and holds an M.Phil. in History and Philosophy of Science from the University of Cambridge. He graduated from Columbia University with a B.S. in Applied Physics and a Minor in Middle Eastern, South Asian, and African Studies.

Too Black to be Arab, too Arab to be Black

Leena Habiballa

Within every Sudanese diasporan is an unceasing internal dialogue about where we fit in the dominant racial order. Sudan is one of the most ethnically, culturally, linguistically and religiously diverse places on the African continent. It was also home to some of the most ancient civilisations in African memory. But today it suffers from the brutal legacy of Arab slavery, Ottoman imperialism and British colonialism. This essay will not attempt to deconstruct this history or examine the ways in which it has shaped the internal racial politics of the country. My focus will instead be on the contemporary Sudanese diasporan experience in the West. This focus does not deny or negate the important and oppressive sociopolitical function of Arab(ised) identity in Sudan and I hope that the more theory-savvy readers will forgive me for the narrow analysis.

My early childhood was spent living in various Arab countries, where I learned from a young age that my darker skin tone threatened my claim to Arabness. To be authentically Arab, it was not enough to speak Arabic or have facets of Arab culture syncretised into my own. My Blackness needed to be invisible. My Arab(ised) identity was, therefore, always contested and fraught, though nevertheless an important part of my being and, ultimately, self-evident. When others denied my Arabness I felt its presence affirmed, for how could something be stripped off if it didn't exist?

It wasn't until my mid to late teens that I was forced to see Blackness and Arabness as ontologically separate. This was the result of being introduced to the Western concept of race. Being racialised within this schema gave me a new sense of self, one which was innately linked to my skin colour and its difference to others. I had previously equated 'Arab' with Arab culture, and 'Black' with skin tone, not an identity. The concept of race, however, meant not only that I now saw Black and Arab as representing very different racial identities but also as invariably competing and mutually exclusive. I had come to embody these two irreconcilable racial categories, and my body became the site of a visceral and daily contradiction.

Too Black to be Arab, too Arab to be Black. This is the daily discourse that I grappled with. I was racially perplexed and traumatised.

My internal conflict was publicly mirrored in the story of Ahmed Mohamed, the 14-year-old prodigy who was racially profiled and arrested in Texas, U.S., for bringing an alleged hoax-bomb to school. Ahmed is a Muslim, Sudanese-American, who has Black African ancestry and Afro-Arab heritage. You would not know this, however, if you listened to the majority of Western voices (including people of colour) who, in the absence of any ethnic subtext, read Ahmed's body as Brown. Online, arguments raged about which Western racial category Ahmed truly embodies. In polemical diatribes many continued the policing of Ahmed's body to define him as either categorically Brown or categorically Black. Lost in all of this is the reality that Western racial constructs and racial politics don't capture the subtleties, complexities, and overlaps of ethnic identities, as with Ahmed.

Being a Sudanese who has fallen victim to this kind of racial policing, I am always curious to see in what ways non-Sudanese react to our racial ambiguity. By racial ambiguity I am not only referring to the colour of one's skin or the texture of one's hair. I am also talking about a person's culture, religious affiliation and heritage. The Sudanese body is a rich and complicated constellation of meaning, a mosaic of identity that is often compromised upon translation into Western racial constructs. The majority of us carry different combinations of African, Arab and Muslim identities, rendering us incoherent to Western racial paradigms. This incoherence makes us suspicious under the globalised racial surveillance of Whiteness. In this sense, Sudanese identities/bodies threaten to harmonise the hierarchical, and therefore irreconcilable, racial dogma that one cannot be more than one thing at a time.

In the past, my Blackness and Arabness shaped my reality in mutually informing, albeit deeply disturbing, ways: the former inspired textbook anti-black racism from non-Black Arabs, who used it as a way of denying me the latter. In contrast, the racial terrain I treaded in the West precluded the very possibility of existing as both. I was in spite of myself, forced to embody alien versions of either Blackness or Arabness, always at the expense of the other. In non-Black, especially Arab, spaces I was read as definitely Black, and in Black spaces I was read as definitely Arab. So real was this daily process of racialisation and racial interrogation that I subconsciously internalised racist Western conceptions of what it means to be 'Arab' and 'Black'. I reproduced them in public spaces as if to perform social scripts with racial sincerity. In non-Black Arab spaces I avoided speaking Arabic for fear of spawning confusion. And in Black spaces, I feared that my Arabness undermined my blackness.

Ultimately, Ahmed's body was racialised as specifically Brown and not Black, and there are (at least) two reasons for this. First, in the context of the so-called US-led War on Terror, the term terrorist circumscribes Muslim and Brown bodies. To justify their indiscriminate bombing across the wider Middle East and North Africa, Brown Muslim bodies must be as broadly defined as possible. It's for that reason that Ahmed, incriminated of terrorism, was profiled by his teachers and the police as a Brown Muslim man, not a Black Muslim boy.

Second, anti-Blackness within Brown and Muslim spaces constructs the victim of Islamophobia as exclusively Brown. To be Black (Muslim) is to be not a real, potential subject of Islamophobia. One ought to ask whether Ahmed's talents would have been so widely celebrated amongst Brown Muslims if he wasn't racially ambiguous enough to fit the few model minority tropes afforded to, say, male South Asian Muslims. Would the same numbers of Muslims and South Asians have shown their solidarity and outrage if Ahmed's Black African heritage were more unambiguously available on his skin?

'But Ahmed himself adopts the label "Brown" to describe his racial identity!' I hear you say. Some have chalked this down to internalised anti-blackness. While this undeniably exists in Sudanese communities, we must distinguish between those instances and the struggle to self-narrate one's body using a social vocabulary that is not one's own. Being Black and Arab diasporans we are expected to communicate the nuances and histories of our bodies through the constraints of a specifically White colonial vocabulary. We fail to traverse the racial landscape because the language available to fuel such a translation is constructed around the White gaze, thereby rendering our attempts at articulation futile. If we do not consider this we risk reifying 'Black', decoupling 'Black' from social construction and using 'Black' in the service of Western cultural imperialism.

In this sense, Ahmed's self-referential use of Brown reflects the struggle to approximate 'Black-Arab' and reconcile Africanness with Arabness. Like all of us, Ahmed has found himself caught trying to navigate a racialised world. The colonial, Western lexicon of race and racism has made it impossible to articulate Black Arab subjectivities. Its vocabulary can't fathom Black-and-Arab except as a racial transgression, as anti-Black racial betrayal or categorical over-spillage to be mopped up, rubbed out, punished and policed whenever possible. It's for that reason that our presence as Black and Arab is unsettling. Our identities are invisible, unthought of and unintelligible to the paradigms of Whiteness.

This failure is also strikingly visible in the coverage of the conflict in Darfur, which has seen an unprecedented wave of destruction and organised violence erupt since 2003. Western media sources, regularly paint the conflict as a race war between Black-Africans and non-Black Arabs. As Prof. Salah Hassan and Dr. Carina Ray point out in Darfur and the Crisis of Governance in Sudan (2008), this locally non-existent racial binary has obfuscated the more complex causes behind the crisis, while revealing the hidden anti-black and anti-Arab bias of the White imaginary. The rhetoric also mirrors trite representations of African wars predicated on primordial identities, in a bid to capitalise on the voyeuristic tendencies of Western populations, including those of non-White folk, who have failed to question this insidious narrative. What makes this distorted framing possible is the preexisting assumption that 'Black' and 'Arab' cannot co-exist in one geographical context, let alone one body.

Non-Black Arabs also operate on and benefit from this separation. They pit their Arabness in direct opposition to Blackness, thereby protecting their claim to Arabness, while gaining proximity to Whiteness.

My experiences and the discussions surrounding Ahmed's body confirm that race is a Western fantasy maintained by a daily, violent socio-political choreography. In an attempt to comprehend Sudanese identity, Western racial classifications construct us as impossible paradoxes, alienating us from our bodies, histories and ways of being. The ever-shifting space between my estranged self and my legitimate self is where my trauma lies, and I will no longer nurture this space.

I refuse to rehearse the logics of race-making or dance to the imperialist drum of racialisation. I will not become digestible to Westerners and non-Black Arabs alike. I will not dilute myself into something you can understand. My complexity is necessary, and it necessitates the abolition of racial orders. I assert Black-Arabness not as a plea to integrate into the race map or gain recognition from an oppressive institution, but to announce that I am here to rattle, shake and disorient a rigid and dogmatic racial hierarchy. I am Black-Arab and I will not uphold a narrative or politics that does not name my reality. I am Black-Arab and I exist.

> *Leena Habiballa is a global soul of Sudanese origin and Co-Editor at Qahwa Project magazine. She graduated with a BSc in (neoliberal) Genetics from University College London in 2014 and is currently pursuing a Postgraduate degree in Genomic Medicine at The University of Manchester.*

Porn: Our Colour Blind Spot When it Comes to Racism

Yomi Adegoke

The general consensus among left-leaning thinkers is that stereotypes, especially harmful, racist ones, are never a good thing. Especially if those stereotypes are being peddled in part for the purposes of sexual gratification and fetishisation. The exception, of course, is when they are solely for sexual gratification and fetishisation.

Then, apparently, it's 'complicated'.

Think piece after think piece on the harms caused by the fetishising of women of colour – on dating sites, in film, in music videos, in theatre, even as statues – flood our timelines with increasing frequency. Yet if the same fetishisation takes place on a porn set, it remains almost entirely bereft of criticism.

In a climate that sees the now supposedly intersectional left (rightfully) call out the fashion industry, the music industry and the film industry for their continued stereotyping of performers of colour, the deafening silence from anti-racist activists regarding racism in porn is hard to comprehend. An adult film seems to be the only place where white people can use the N-word with wild abandon and without fear of backlash – and there doesn't seem to be a rationale as to why this is acceptable.

Several rather unconvincing arguments have been put forward for why porn receives the protection from criticism other forms of media do not. The first is consent – performers involved have consented to partaking in these acts and films, however racist they may be, and therefore any criticism of the films is rendered redundant.

'I think real racism is awful, just like real incest and real rape, but interracial porn is just as much a fantasy as those other genres', porn actress Casey Calvert explained to Mic.com when asked about her thoughts regarding porn's race-baiting. And for many, her commentary remains sufficient reason to remain schtum. But the issue of the consent of performers has never stopped the voicing of valid concerns and critique in the past or present.

2014 saw the cancellation of controversial 'Exhibit B' by South African artist Brett Bailey. His installation featured black actors in shackles and chains in order – he claimed – to 'confront European notions of racial supremacy and the current plight of immigrants'. After a #boycottthehumanzoo campaign garnering 20,000 signatures and a protest outside the venue, it was called off, much to the ire of the participants.

'Sometimes you come across a piece and just go, "That's it! That's exactly what I want to say." We all really saw this as a journey, as a way of changing things', performer Priscilla Adade-Helledy told Vice News. 'We were being totally unvoiced by the people who said they were anti-racists. It was really depressing.'

Similarly, Lily Allen's questionable 2013 single 'Hard out Here' saw Allen sneer at scantily clad black and Asian dancers, panning over their buttocks as she sang lines such as 'Don't need to shake my ass for you 'cause I've got a brain'. Whilst the backlash from critics was severe, those involved saw things differently: 'Critics will be critics', dancer Monique Lawrence tweeted. 'Lily Allen is the coolest, most down to earth and we all had a blast shooting!'

When the consent of the performers is present in situations such as these, instances of racism have still been called out – especially when (as with the above two incidents), the individual in the driving seat is white. But it's difficult to fathom how criticism of Lily Allen's music video is so widespread while a porn parody of Eric Garner's death, alongside an adult film entitled 'Black Wives Matter' 'satirising' the Black Lives Matter movement leaves so-called social justice warriors silent. Why does the consent of performers only seem to matter when there is an erection at stake?

In Critical Dialogues in Cultural Studies, Stuart Hall articulated the point that different types of media representation of minority groups have important and wide-spanning effects, including the reinforcement of existing stereotypes. Whether or not this reinforcement takes place depends on the historical and social context that the media in question is received in, rather than the intent, or indeed consent of those who create it. So porn performers, like actors and musicians, have no control over the potentially negative ramifications of the representations they have individually consented to participating in.

Currently, there is more vocal criticism of blockbusters

than of blue films. Ridley Scott's Gods of Egypt was heavily chastised for its decision to cast black characters in offensive roles. One can't help but think whether a porn parody of the film featuring the exact same roles would be somewhat more palatable? After all, a porn version of an already racist blockbuster would appear to have less of a chance, by current logic, of being seen as politically 'problematic'.

A variety of the worst, most harmful tropes are used and amplified within porn: tropes that we are steadily attempting to get rid of from the big screen for good. The submissive Asian woman, the spicy Latina and sassy black woman that we're gradually pushing out of the mainstream continue to have a home on porn sites. And just like mainstream films, the majority of those at the production end of mainstream porn are white men – though that doesn't seem to bother many within this context.

Orientalism, othering and white supremacy are rife and at times, central themes. 'Watch these latin putas gag on white guys cocks in the most abusive throatjobs you will ever see!' one site called 'Latina Abuse' shouts. Titles such as 'Two Hot Black Men Get Jiggy and Wild, Robbery Style', 'The Heiress' Black Slave Boy', 'Ebony Cum Dumps', 'Exploited Black Teens', 'Exploited Africans', 'Teen Slaves of Saigon' and 'Raped By Arab Terrorists' litter X rated sites all over the web. The usually critical voices remain silent.

There appears to be no concern that actors such as Lebanese-American Mia Khalifa's appeal plays on orientalist and xenophobic tropes. As blogger Mira Abouelezz so eloquently puts it, 'It is a white fantasy in which the agency of brown people is taken away. The brown woman has no voice or real identity, she just symbolizes something 'Other' to be conquered.'

The practice in which characters belonging to a marginalised group are played by those who do not share their identity in real life has been increasingly objected to, especially when the portrayals are likely to cause offense to those in the relevant community. Mia Khalifa, for instance, who often performs scenes in a hijab, is not a Muslim and claims that these performances are 'satirical'. It is difficult to imagine that the same practices could be so silently accepted within any other medium. Yet supposed allies appear sated by the ever-present idiom 'It's not racist, it's just a fetish!', suggesting that the two are mutually exclusive. A 'Hi there Beyoncé' or Rihanna, or Nicki — or another black pop cultural icon you bear absolutely no resemblance to — message on Tinder is considered a micro-aggression of epic proportions. But if the same man then decides to go home and masturbate over the very fetishising that saw you swiftly block him from Tinder, to challenge him would be kink shaming. Just how is it possible to object to fetishisation in every other conceivable context, but then ignore or even accept it in pornography?

The double standard at play is that racial denigration is supposedly somehow neutralised by the sexual element as opposed to exacerbated by it. Writer Jamel Shabbaz describes a scene from the popular site Ghetto Gaggers, of which violent racial subjugation is the primary selling point:

'During 90 minutes of barbarism, the perpetrators spit in their faces, slap them, stomp them and force some to crawl on all fours with chains around their necks. In other scenes, the women have watermelons smashed on their heads and then are forced to eat the melon, along with the men's semen. There are now hundreds of sites specializing in the sexual destruction of the "ghetto bitch".'

A now defunct site called NaziNiggers showed white men in Nazi gear physically assaulting black women. The Mandingo, thug and sex pest stereotypes that have seen black men targeted and slain in real life remain central. And scenes primarily hinge on white supremacy, neo-colonialism and bigotry without challenge.

Alex Pesek writes about one site, 'Thug Hunters', which sees white men scouring the most deprived parts of cities 'to find black men willing to fellate them for cash'.

'We found a thug wandering the rough streets of Miami', describes one of the studio's hunts for a black man, as if he wasn't a human but a creature in his natural habitat. 'We ... fed him dreams of money, bitches, stardom (sic) and rap songs sung in his honour and he was like sweet milk chocolate in our hand'. Pesek notes that it is such real-life racialised power dynamics that appeal to most of its viewers. And that makes me profoundly uncomfortable.

'But it's just a fantasy!' detractors will huff. Yet, even if that is true, isn't almost all the media we consume? Is a Lily Allen music video somehow more real than a porn film? Is an exhibition? Other 'fantasy worlds' – fashion, film — that peddle the same argument as a means of absolving them of any real world responsibility are immediately dismissed as sub-par attempts to excuse bigotry.

As with porn, pleasure can be taken from viewing any politically 'problematic' media. But most are not exempt from a critical analysis of why they are enjoyed and how what they represent may still be harmful. Many viewers took offense to Chris Rock and Ali G's racially-insensitive recent speeches at the Oscars – but others responded with stock arguments that 'what we find funny is involuntary'. The same is said of what turns us on, but certain strands of the modern left only remain broadly critical of one. A porn webseries called 'Border Patrol Sex' made light of the rape of migrant Mexican and Central American women – if it had been a comedy skit on SNL, the outrage would have been widespread.

Fantasies do not form within a vacuum but are shaped by a world that we all know is violently misogynistic and racist. Racist scenarios remain pervasive fantasies first and foremost because they are based on deeply-entrenched social structures, stereotypes and power dynamics. And whilst minorities may indulge in these fantasies too, it takes an alarming level of intellectual dishonesty to suggest that that this somehow negates racism while at the same time ignoring racism among the primary creators and consumers of these particular products. The Ghetto Gaggers twitter account recently tweeted the message 'Merry Christmas! #BlackLivesMatter remember that in this time of joy', accompanied by an image of a black woman being double penetrated by two white men, whilst holding up a sign reading Black Lives Matter – it's not hard to imagine what it's creators' politics are.

Liberal sites are not, admittedly, entirely silent on the issue of racism in porn and have written about how it is manifested between actors, the pay gap and in categorisation – but never regarding the content. The story of porn actor James Deen's (who has had a number of sexual assault allegations made against him by female colleagues) trouble casting women opposite black male performers made every site imaginable. There have been write ups of how black female performers are continually short-changed. The perceived taboo of interracial/cuckolding scenes is constantly discussed but the nature of the scenes, and thus the actual product, is never interrogated. Where there is any attempt to do so, only half-hearted justifications are offered. Mike Stabile and Jack Judah Shamama, owners of Gay Porn Blog acknowledge that porn has 'strains of racism' but argue that so do 'politics, so does larger culture.'

'If you're looking for racism, you'll find it – that's what free speech is about. Sometimes it's ugly, but it's wrong to paint with too broad a brush', Stabile continues. A left led by student groups — who are now being characterised as the natural enemies of free speech — have somehow found themselves in bed with the very 'Je suis Charlie' advocates they usually abhor.

Meanwhile porn actor Mickey Mod recently discussed the unequal labour practices that take place within the industry, stating, 'America consumes race-based content because it has a long way to go in dealing with race issues, but that content doesn't have to be made in a racist way'. If Hollywood were to vastly increase the ethnic diversity of both actors and directors in Hollywood, along with their pay cheques but still churn out the same stereotypical, offensive and overtly racist films, I wonder if it would be considered a step forward. As Stuart Hall made clear, 'films are not necessarily good because black people make them.' In every other industry we interrogate and critique both the institutional structures and the output but whilst some of the shortcomings in porn are addressed, the issues regarding what we are actually viewing are not.

A minority of BAME women actors are now creating and managing their own less racist product. Although these women have been continually wheeled out as evidence of a changing porn landscape, this type of rationale is no more satisfactory than saying Hollywood isn't racist because Ava Duvernay exists or that there is no issue within modelling because of the success of Naomi Campbell. It feels like most of the other arguments: an unapologetically neoliberal rationalisation. Focusing heavily on a small number of exceptions without acknowledging that they are exceptions and not the rule is usually the tactic of our hard-right detractors. We don't accept these arguments anywhere else – why would we in porn?

There are real tensions regarding race and porn that have not been addressed critically, and the unwillingness to do so openly and honestly is deeply disappointing. Highlighting the problematic representations and power relationships within the porn industry is not anti-porn. I have yet to come across a convincing argument as to why porn should be excluded from critical analysis. A sex-positive stance should not mean an inability to stand against the blatant racism in porn along with all its other problems, or an indifference to the experiences of those who work within the sex industry.

'Contemporary portrayals of Black women [and men] in pornography represent the continuation of the historical treatment of their actual bodies', Patricia Hill Collins explains in her book Black Feminist Thought. When will critical thinkers and activists begin to openly acknowledge this without reverting to apologism for an industry that continues to degrade, exploit and ultimately mock us?

Yomi Adegoke is a writer from Croydon. She writes primarily about politics, pop culture, race, feminism and how they intersect. When she's not writing, she likes to read about the stuff she likes to writes about, as well as paint and travel.

'Her Nose was Straight with a Soft Tip at the End' — Writing Race at School

Clare Warner

The set texts for GCSE English literature still strongly favour the works of Anglo-British novelists, poets and playwrights above all others. Although many educators and academics have rightly critiqued the Eurocentrism of the National Curriculum, few studies have attempted to demonstrate and quantify the impact on students of a Eurocentric curriculum, which is the purpose of this article. My research examined the way Year 10 students from a South London state school constructed whiteness and non-whiteness in the short stories they submitted. The findings and the implications for curriculum reform are discussed.

The school is an inner city school in south London. The pupils live in wards with the highest levels of social and economic deprivation. Like many such schools it has a diverse intake with a rich mix of ethnic and cultural groups. Over 50 languages are spoken at the school. I have used the broad and imperfect terms 'White' and 'Non-White' to reflect the way students in the study are socially understood by both the students and society at large. Both groups are diverse with the latter including those with Caribbean, African, South American, South and East Asian and Southern European heritage. The sample that I will talk about consists of 35 stories taken from two Year 10 classes, a high achieving and a less able group. Five students in the sample were white and the rest non-white as defined here. Of the 30 non-white students roughly one third were born outside the UK and had experience of another educational system.

The Study

In preparing students for GCSE English literature, I set an original writing task which fulfilled coursework requirements. The task was based on students' study of the set literature text Of Mice and Men by John Steinbeck. In the novel Steinbeck employs a formulaic structure, launching each chapter with a brief description followed by dialogue. Based on this structure, I set students the task of creating an opening for a short story. But first we reviewed how to create settings, characters and dialogue effectively. I deliberately exposed students to literature set in diverse settings including a mosque and a black hair salon, in the hope that they would begin to think widely about the possibilities for their stories. The only requirement was that they relinquish the preferred use of the first person (I) in favour of the third person approach as this affords limitless possibilities for creating points of view within a narrative structure. The tasks' emphasis on creating settings and characters inevitably engaged students in making decisions and arguably articulating worldviews about how people are positioned according to their race, class and gender.

Power and Privilege as Whiteness

Over half the non-white students (17) and all five white students in the study created white characters. This suggests that students opted to replicate the narratives they encountered through their study of literature instead of creating narratives centred on their lived experience. As a social category whiteness was viewed by both white and non-white students as one of power and privilege. A Caribbean-born student encapsulates this in her description of the home-based office of a white professional, Mrs. Bradley. She notes that the office was 'strewn with books' and that 'On the baige (sic) painted walls hung four qualification certificates with marble frames'. Professionalism in the story is associated with high educational attainment and with being white. On several occasions, students also positioned their white characters as powerful in relation to less powerful non-white or white working class characters. Mangan (1993) argues that the curriculum is a specific medium for expressing political relationships, and a demonstration of the distribution of power in society. The students generally demonstrated an awareness of these power differences along racial lines but had neither a critique nor an understanding of how that power is both acquired and upheld.

One student of West African descent demonstrated this in her creation of two South American characters, Carlos and Rosetta, who sit on a beach and discuss the difficulties of being together when their parents disapprove of their relationship. Across the street from the beach she describes 'the glistening five star hotel'. She makes passing reference to the 'rich guests with an endless stream of colourful cocktails' who, unlike Carlos and Rosetta are unracialised and are therefore assumed to be white (a common practice in GCSE literature set texts). The pair look on at the glamorous lifestyle they are excluded from. Although she offers this depiction, she fails to critique the racial hierarchy which excludes Carlos and Rosetta from accessing the hotel because the category of rich tourist is fixed as white.

A student who arrived from Nigeria in September wrote a story set in Nigeria in which local people are relegated to the background in favour of European characters. She begins by creating a tropical setting: 'The wind was shaking the rusty fingers of palm-leaves'. She evokes the summer sounds: the 'frog voices, and the grating cicadas', and the 'ever present pulse of music from the neighbouring native huts'. She describes it all as though she is an outsider. Implicit in her description is a judgement which positions the 'natives' and their 'huts' as inferior to the main – white – characters who occupy a bungalow. The characters Jerry and Francis are 'white in complexion'. They are later described as 'two Englishmen', producing Englishness as synonymous with being white.

Her story seems to confirm Nandy's (1983) contention that 'the West is now everywhere, within the West and outside; in structures and in minds' (quoted in Mangan, p. 6). In creating these narratives, students demonstrate their acceptance of a racialised social hierarchy which positions them, the non-white or working class white students, as at the bottom of the pile. The danger is that the worldview presented to students through the curriculum and reproduced in their narratives presents the social hierarchy as fixed and unchangeable, thereby restricting them to a limited script for their lives.

Eurocentric Ideas about Beauty

In addition to assigning power and privilege to white characters, non-white students also imbued them with signifiers of beauty which were wholly oppositional to their own physical beings. One story by a student of Nigerian descent featured a character described as 'a very attractive young lady'. The author continues, 'she had long brown hair that hung from her head in loose curls, big bright light brown eyes that sparkled, a pointy very bony nose.' A student of Egyptian descent introduced the central character in her narrative as follows: 'A fetching woman entered the room. She had porcelain white skins (sic) with bright cherry lips.' A Turkish girl described '25 year old Valentina whose lavish hair was tinted with blond streaks. Her nose was straight with a soft tip at the end'. An Asian student in a story ominously titled 'Popular', about a friendship group at an American high school, described the beautiful leader of the group Tina as 'a tall girl with deep blue eyes and long blond hair' and her rival Cindy as having 'straight blond hair and medium sized blue eyes'. A Caribbean heritage student created a white character, Desiree, whose very name conjures up notions of being desired and desirable. Desiree has 'long honey blond hair which resembled the sand on a beach'. We learn that 'she takes after a Barbie doll, with her perfect hair, manicured nails and fashion designer clothes.' Although there were only three blond girls in the study group, blond was the descriptor most often used in relation to beauty, revealing the power of the cultural ideology, often upheld through curriculum choices which link beauty to whiteness.

Stereotypes

When the students did create ethnically diverse characters, they often relied on negative stereotypes. In contrast to the wealth and decadence of the worlds inhabited by white characters, non-white characters were generally shown as disadvantaged. One student of African descent describes how Michelle, a white woman, is followed by a man through a park on her way home after a night out. The student creates a tense atmosphere, foreshadowing a bad outcome. The piece ends abruptly with a confrontation between the two characters. We learn nothing of the man except that he is 'dark of face', which reinscribes mainstream ideas about the black man as a threat to social order. Arguably, the student's lack of critical consciousness about race makes her powerless to do anything other than recreate the very stereotypes which position her as inferior. Her lack of critical consciousness makes her complicit in her own subjugation.

Two other students of African and of Caribbean descent both wrote narratives about young black female characters who experience unplanned pregnancy. The character in one of the stories reveals her pregnancy to her boyfriend. His brutal response is 'You're telling me like I care. Get an abortion innit? It's not my problem. Whatever. Phone me when you get rid of it'. The narrative presents a distorted and dysfunctional relationship between a young black man and woman in strong contrast to the numerous love stories submitted in which idyllic love is described between white characters.

Three students of African descent wrote stories featuring robberies committed by non-white characters. One was set in a dark alleyway covered in litter and graffiti and populated by stray cats. Into the alleyway walks 'a young girl

with dark chocolate skin'. The girl, we learn, is on her way
to meet her friend (another young black girl) to rob an audio-
visual store, reinforcing the stereotype of black youth having
a proclivity for crime. When questioned informally about these
choices, many students insisted that in their stories they were
merely reproducing social reality. Yet most students have little
consciousness of how the media shapes the perception of
that reality and how systems of oppression including racism,
sexism and classism create disadvantaged social realities.
Without this knowledge they have little choice but to reproduce
stereotypes in their narratives and potentially in their lives.

In Black and White

Although the young people inhabit multiracial spaces
in their neighbourhoods and schools, only three submissions
featured a multiracial cast of characters – further evidence
of the divide between the students' realities and their written
narratives. This tendency towards homogeneity is reflected
in the contemporary English curriculum in which the social
realities covered in the literature texts studied are generally
either wholly white or positioned oppositionally as wholly non-
white. This is most clearly apparent in the poetry unit titled
'Poems from Other Cultures and Traditions' (my emphasis).

Where students did create spaces shared by diverse
characters, they invariably positioned the characters as
being oppositional and often in conflict with each other. One
student's story featured a black prisoner, Jennifer. The story
focuses on a conflict that ensues between Jennifer, a seasoned
black prisoner, and a white newcomer, Louise. The two women
are presented as at opposite ends of the spectrum in looks
and persona. Jennifer's 'mahogany skin' is contrasted with
Louise's 'white skin which seemed to go paler'. While Louise
has 'unclean blond hair and blue eyes', Jennifer wears a
'midnight coloured weave'. Throughout the story Jennifer acts
aggressively towards Louise, speaking directly and bluntly.
Louise is presented as timid, as evident from her stammering
responses to Jennifer's interrogation. The student's story
reveals a common tendency to think about race through
opposing categories of black and white. This fuels the creation
of stereotypes that, in this instance, surround black and
white femininity.

One student of Nigerian descent chose to describe an
inter-racial marriage between a black woman, Marian, and
a white man, Peter. She describes the couple's living room
firstly as Afrocentric by referencing the 'textile cushions,

dark coffee brown palate, pieces of African art, the masks carved of Ancient African Kings', then goes on to describe the white Western influences in the room which include a 'silver legged glass table'. Along with these stylistic features, the characters themselves are also presented as opposites. Marian is described as 'a petite toffee coloured black woman in an African tunic', whereas Peter is 'a tall elegant white man with dark denim jeans and shiny black loafers'. Although the student falls prey to this dualistic convention of representation, she also transcends it by presenting a tender exchange between the two characters. More than any of the other students, she demonstrates how writing can produce insights into social life, as well as providing a means to imagine and reorder the world differently. Arguably, in order for more students to experience the practice of writing as liberatory, they would need to be engaged in critical dialogue about the social and historical construction of race, among other identities. This would enable them to move beyond doing no more than reproducing the racialised narratives they are exposed to through the curriculum and the media.

Knowing Differently

Antiracist educator Dei (1996) argues that through the school's curriculum, educators and students are provided with academic definitions of what counts as valid knowledge. It is not unfeasible to think that by the time non-white and working class white students reach Year 10, their experience of the education system has taught them that their lives are unsuitable to be the content of literature. The students' submissions reinforce the idea that personal knowledge exists as separate from the official body of knowledge, and this undoubtedly alienates pupils from school and education at large. Taken together, the students' writing reveals the power of the formal curriculum to shape worldviews. It also raises urgent questions about how schools are failing to equip students with the necessary skills to navigate modern British society by refusing to introduce critical discussions about gender, race and class into the curriculum.

A version of this essay originally appeared in Race Equality Teaching, Trentham Books 2009

Clare Warner is an FE lecturer and PhD student in the educational studies department at Goldsmiths. She is currently researching the experiences of African-Caribbean practitioners/organisations in applying to open Free Schools. She is a critical race theory enthusiast and uses the framework to help her think through issues of race and racism and their intersection with class and gender in the history, policy and practice of education.

References

Dei, G. (1996) Anti-racism Education: Theory and Practice, Halifax: Fernwood Publishing.

Mangan, J.A. (1993) 'Images for Confident Control: Stereotypes in Imperial Discourse' in Mangan, J.A. (Ed)

The Imperial Curriculum: Racial Images and education in the British Colonial Experience, New York: Routledge Nandy, A. (1983)

The Intimate Enemy: Loss and Recovery of Self under Colonialism, New Delhi: Oxford University Press

'Integration' or 'Assimilation' is a Two-sided Negotiation

Chimene Suleyman

A much older cousin lived in London's Turkish neighbourhood of Green Lanes for forty years, and never learnt to speak English. She earned money tailoring clothes from a sewing machine in her living room. She shopped in local stores owned and frequented by other Turks. She socialised with her family. There was —as she saw it— little urgency for another language. In fact, there was little time. Above all, she had raised two children to speak English perfectly, have English friends, and to contribute to British society with good jobs in IT and wins at martial-art championships.

Attributing blame to a woman who does not learn the language of a country is as good as forgetting we are not the sum of every ambition life got in the way of. Being a working mother of two will almost certainly "get in the way". Depression and social nervousness, ever present, will play their part.

The first four months of moving to New York, I could barely bring myself to speak to anyone despite advantage of a shared language. I arrived with a partner whose company made moving as easy as possible. It was also my choice. I moved, not from an abusive financial economy or war, but simply because I was bored. Nonetheless, migrating was a grief; a despondency which consumes, born of the separation from everyone I have ever loved. We had started again; moving to a house that wouldn't feel like home, finding our feet in the buzz of someone else's (albeit familiar) culture, amid the overwhelming loneliness of it all. To think, there are only two of us, not young children in tow. If it had been demanded that during this already difficult adjustment, I had to learn, say, Russian on top of it, this may have been too much.

So unresolved is the value of integration, that there has been no such thing as an agreed global technique, nor expectation of our response to a move. I repeat sentences in my accent to impressed Americans, explaining phrases and slang until they parrot them back to me. Grateful for new words and information —which shows do I watch? Can I recommend British music in turn? Assimilation here is two-sided.

The most powerful motif of integration always seem to belong to those communities who have replicated a home away from home; the Indians in Southall, the Caribbeans in Tottenham and Peckham, the Greeks in Edmonton, the Jews in Golders Green. This is not rigid self-governing, nor division, rather the fluidity of continuity. Likewise, they cannot exist without the understanding and reverence of the host nation, whose own culture widens and benefits simply by accommodating.

Simply put, the only rule is acceptance, which is a must from both communities who mix like a kind of venn diagram until there is something of its own in the middle. However, £20m fund so immigrant women may learn English bears none of this. A worthy idea placed in a box of razors. After two and half years, women on a spousal visa will be tested on language. On failing, she will be faced with deportation. Young Muslim men, David Cameron said, are susceptible to radicalisation because Muslim women cannot speak out against Imams. Muslim women, he believes, can learn English to help their sons from turning to extremism. So strong is the control of fear that foresight and evidence are neither provided nor necessary. The existence of Daesh has become enough in Britain to simply imagine outcomes and separate women from their children.

The denial of humanity is to see a woman who speaks only her mother-tongue and blame it on her religion. It is to forget that she too experiences the very same every-day chores, stresses, and distractions that have limited us all in some way. She is given one narrative —a procedure of white supremacy— in which black boys who wear hoods cannot be cold, nor fashionable, but are "thugs"; where Jewish business owners are not hard-working contributors to the economy but instead greedy and miserly; where Muslim women who do not speak English are complicit in acts of terrorism, not people who are busy or mentally ill-prepared to retain a new language.

No matter. There is nothing new in throwing accusations of terrorism at Islam and hoping something sticks. On explaining why Muslim women were singled out in a plan considered for all non-English speaking women, a government source said, "David knows that the traditional submissiveness of Muslim women is a sensitive issue [...] At the moment, too many Muslim women are treated like second-class citizens who may speak only basic English at best, and have no jobs or independent financial standing."

Credible reasoning cannot be found in a statement that relies so heavily on "they all look the same". The way of life for a Muslim woman in Saudi Arabia will differ from that of a woman in Turkey, who in turn will differ from that of a woman in Eritrea, and so on. That is to say, there is nothing theocratically traditional about submission; rather, it is a varying product of nationality. In fact, when it comes to gender, it is worth remembering that "women as second-class citizens" is maintained worldwide.

But the portrait of Muslim men as patriarchal appeals in a way that white men controlling a woman's modesty — we have all known the man who has met his partner's outfit on a girls' night out with rage; we are heavily aware of a jurisdiction that believes the length of a woman's skirt may contribute to her rape — or her financial stability (the pay-gap) does not. The one who cares about the well-being of women will not do so only within the parameters of criticising Islam. Domestic violence refuges have closed at such a rate under Cameron's government that vulnerable women and children have been put back 40 years. A woman is killed by a man every two days in Britain, a statistic that is not likely to reduce any time soon. Every year 85,000 women are raped in England and Wales, where 97 per cent of these see no justice. Submission is submission, no matter the language —or two — a woman speaks.

Now consider this: since the Paris attacks, violence against Muslims has increased 300 per cent, where the vast majority of its victims are women. Muslim women have spoken for some years of being spat at, hit, or having their veils pulled from their bodies by white men in public spaces. If we had reached the denouement of integration and its value, we would know that in order for it to work it must be reciprocal. Offering English to non-speakers would then share a platform, say, with a project to unteach white men the kind of bigotry that manifests in violence.

Only understanding the use of Muslim women as props can explain how there may be concern for a woman's wellbeing around brown men, but not white. Why this plan does not target all failing participants of a harmonised society has yet to be asked. There is, unfortunately, real danger of extreme behaviour from a man who grows loathsome of a country that defamed his mother, then separated her from him as a child. Never because of the language she loved him in.

Chimene Suleyman is a writer from London. She has written about race for Media Diversified, The Independent, IBTimes, The Pool, The Debrief, to a name a few. She has appeared on BBC Newsnight and BBC radio. She is a contributing essayist to best selling book The Good Immigrant, and her poetry collection Outside Looking On was featured in a Guardian's Best Books of 2014 list. She currently lives in New York.

Breaking Tongues: Carrying Names Across Borders

Sinthujan Varatharajah

I was named Sinthujan, a holy river for Hindus that in today's Pakistan kills hundreds during the floods. However, neither that river, its Sanskrit origin or the subcontinent's partition really mattered to my parents. Sinthuja is a common Tamil name given to girls. It's a name that has survived decolonisation and nationalism's drive for linguistic purification. It also survived war and flight. My parents used it to communicate as forbidden penpals while racial conflicts were unfolding around them. Sinthuja is the name my father used to hide his male and 'untouchable' origin. It connected riversides, divided societies but also caste apartheid. Upon my birth in exile, they altered the name to suit my gender ascription and added an extra 'n'. Besides also unbordering genders, my name also connected me to a lost homeland where it could have identified me as a future 'terrorist'.

At home I quickly became Sinthu, an endearing (female) name used by relatives and later also white friends who struggled to pronounce my full name. My community, on the other hand, struggled to get over its gender bending. It caused confusions and giggles. Patriarchy was challenged by my name in ways they weren't used to yet. Outside of it, it was easier to provide white friends with my pet name than to teach them my actual name and watch their tongues struggle with its unfamiliarity. Rather than expecting them to pronounce my name with the same softness and delicacy in which it was given to me, I wanted to simplify it for them. My name stood out as it was. I didn't want them to also know about its gender ambiguity, or its cultural cosmologies. When I moved to London, I tried to return to my birth name as the opportunity arose in my early adult life to create a new name-based identity in a new landscape. I still sometimes opted to allow certain friends to call me Sinthu as it provided a sense of intimacy and familiarity in London's then unfamiliar boroughs.

At some point in my life, without me even realising it, some white people, including university lecturers, started calling me 'Sinth'. They pronounced the 'th' not as a soft 'd' as Tamil would require it, but as an English 'th'. It was an alteration that I had never encountered or even imagined as possible. I felt colonized. My initial shock and anger were quickly replaced by resignation as to how our bodies and cultures, including our names can be subjugated. Born into a Western dominated world, my name after all was always at risk, something that was not necessarily mine. In similar ways to my body, it was up for negotiation. When you grow up with phrases like 'Do you go by any other name?' on meeting new people, you acclimatise to appreciating even small, albeit problematic or clumsy attempts, to call you by your birth name. Thank you for trying, thank you for seeing me, thank you for leaving me with five of my name's original nine letters.

Later on, some white people thought that my already butchered name was still too long and complicated. They reduced me to nothing more than 'Sin'. 'Sin'. In their attempts to make my name sound familiar, they cut it to what was not just remotely relatable, but a term quite literally taken from their vocabulary. And an unfortunate word at that. Known territory also provided a translation they could work with – but I couldn't. My foreign name was no more foreign. At the end of it, it was no longer my name anymore. I wasn't sure how to react to it, how to express my frustration and resistance without being called 'angry' or 'dramatic', without being that man of colour who sees racism and power everywhere. When you are born with nine letters and watch how you, over a short time span, are reduced to no more than three, you wonder what you'll be left with upon death – if anything will remain of you.

The name that I was given came with sounds, senses and feelings, many of which are positioned outside of western semiotics. The name was a cache for memories, lost histories and songs. Its tenderness has been slowly hollowed out, its context rendered irrelevant, its written form erased. Its sensual and acoustic properties were given no space or form in which to survive in western landscapes as they were. They weren't representable, neither in discourse or practice, but required modification in order to become pronounceable, representable – and real. The meaning my parents ascribed to my name, its racial and caste histories and gender tensions, the meaning derived from cultures that surpass western civilisation, how my name felt and sounded in their mouths were by the end of it no more. Just as the river I was named after is not known by its local name in the West, I was destined not to be known by my actual name.

The act of naming has always been deeply political. The way our names are spoken and treated says something about how our racialised and othered bodies, as well as our cultural cosmologies, are positioned and treated in the everyday. The way our names are grinded between the teeth of others, its letters torn apart by their tongues and reassembled in their throats, is political. This process of gradual erasure or modification falls within a larger history of how we are perceived, constructed and positioned, and how the onus of labour is put on us to acquiesce and to become accustomed to how power can flatten our differences and colonise our bodies and identities, against our own self-determination and aspirations. These are the power dynamics that render so many of us to shorten our names, to westernise them or to replace them with Western ones to build bridges to the hemisphere that prevents us to exist as we are. The alterations of our names are an erasure, a theft of culture and negation of complexities. They are colonialism. To have a name is a privilege, just as it is to be given the dignity to be addressed the way we choose to be.

Sinthujan Varatharajah is a doctoral student in Political Geography at University College London, University, He holds a Masters in Race, Ethnicity and Postcolonial Studies from the London School of Economics and Political Science and is the founder of Roots of Diaspora, a multimedia storytelling project on refugeehood and migration.

No Reconciliation without Recognition: A Personal History of the Armenian Genocide

Robert Kazandjian

On April 24, 2015 Armenians worldwide commemorated the centenary of the Armenian Genocide. In 1915, Ottoman authorities arrested approximately 250 prominent Armenian community figures and intellectuals in Constantinople, the majority of whom were executed. The great poet Daniel Varoujan was disembowelled before his eyes were gouged out. The carnage spread like a malignancy across the land; cultural leaders were rounded up and murdered, silencing voices of resistance and leaving communities vulnerable to attack. Tens of thousands of able-bodied Armenian men serving in the Ottoman Army were forced to disarm, transferred to labour battalions and then butchered by bayonet or gunshot while performing work duties. Wholesale deportation of all Armenians from Eastern Anatolia to concentration camps in the scorching Syrian Desert was ordered. Deportation was code for massacre. Men, women and children were slaughtered. The barbaric methodology varied. Those who survived the death marches were left to starve in the camps. One and a half million lives were lost.

Fuelled by a pan-Turkic ideology, the chauvinist nationalist wing of the Young Turk Movement, under the banner of the Committee of Union and Progress, planned and conducted the Armenian Genocide. The First World War created ideal conditions for systematic annihilation to take place, allowing the Armenian minority to be cast as a threat to national security. Mustafa Kemal Ataturk's modern Turkish republic, soaring from the ashes of the Ottoman Empire, was built on the myth of resistance against the imperial powers. The truth was that his immediate predecessors had expunged minority peoples from their homeland, creating the monolithic state Ataturk desired. Kemalists initiated the vehement denial of the genocide, refusing to acknowledge that large Armenian communities ever existed in Turkey. Propaganda depicted the Armenian minority as a rebellious, violent insurgency and attributed deaths to internal conflict. This has been the Turkish governmental line of argument from Ataturk to Erdogan.

Coupled with the ideological reasons behind the Turkish state's perpetual denial of the Armenian genocide are the practical reasons. Recognition of the genocide would strengthen the argument for reparations to be paid to the families of Armenians who had property expropriated and redistributed by the Ottoman government. If Turkey were deemed to bear legal responsibility for the meticulously calculated theft that took place, the financial implications would be monumental.

The politics in this context have a deeply personal foundation for all Armenians. This is not just about history. This is about our lives, our identities, and our very existence. I have previously written of how our battle for recognition and against denial continues. I have addressed the wounds inflicted upon our collective consciousness from a safe distance, occupying myself with the big picture. However, when I consider the details of my own family's survival of the genocide, the unrelenting weight of history becomes too much to bear. It is when I pause and reflect on their suffering that I feel the blade of the Ottoman gendarme's bayonet wedged between my own shoulder blades.

My father, Armenag, first son of Vahe and Rebecca Kazandjian, was born in Cairo in 1951. He carries the middle name of Abraham, in honour of his maternal grandfather, Abraham Tudjarian. The holy city of Urfa was the birthplace of the prophet Abraham/Ibrahim. In the 5th century, Mesrop Mashtots created the Armenian alphabet there, signalling the dawn of Armenian literature and ensuring the survival of our ancestors as a distinct people. On the eve of the genocide, Urfa was home to the Tudjarian family and 45,000 other Armenians. In the scorching summer of 1915, Ottoman soldiers arrived at the Tudjarians' property.

Abraham was 6 years old and the youngest of 4 brothers. His parents were taken away. He would never again play backgammon with his mother. He would never again feel his father's kiss on his forehead. The soldiers returned. Abraham's brothers suggested that as he was so small and slight, he hide in the barn. The older boys insisted that no matter what he heard or saw, Abraham must remain hidden amongst the straw. Cowering in his hiding place, Abraham looked on as his brothers' young lives ended beneath the shade of olive trees.

Abraham conquered the terror that gripped him, emerging from the barn a day or two after his brothers were murdered. He stumbled through the broken, bloody ruins of his community. On the brink of exhaustion, Abraham was offered shelter and warmth by a Turkish family who were repulsed by the Ottoman government's brutal campaign. From there he was sent to one of many orphanages for Armenian children in Greece. One imagines this decision was made with his safety in mind, given the fervour and fanaticism with which the genocide was undertaken. In total, orphanages in Greece became sanctuaries for around 15,000 Armenian children. It was in this safe space that Abraham would meet Ovssana, a fellow orphan from Urfa. We know nothing of the trauma she endured, of the horrors her childish eyes witnessed. Armenian women often carried the burden of their suffering in silence. Patriarchy created the space for misplaced shame, meaning the sexual abuse that took place during the genocide was seldom discussed openly. United in grief, the two would eventually fall in love, only to be separated when Ovssana joined relatives in Cairo who had escaped the killing.

At the age of 18, Abraham embarked on the pursuit of happiness and followed his soulmate to Egypt, only to discover that she had been coerced into marrying an older man. Armenian culture was, and still is, steeped in patriarchal attitudes, and this hideous practice was not uncommon. The star-crossed pair would not be denied, lobbying Ovssana's family until the forced union was annulled. My great-grandparents, orphaned by the genocide, were finally joined in marriage. Together they had 8 children, one of whom was my grandmother, Rebecca. Perhaps it was written by the gods that my great grandfather was never supposed to live a long life; he contracted gastro-enteritis and died at the age of 42. Abraham's body succumbed to illness during the months preceding my father's birth. Armenag would never be held by the man to whom he ultimately owes his existence.

I find it painfully humbling that I too am here because of Abraham's bravery, because he didn't cry out in terror when he witnessed his siblings' throats being cut. I am here because of the selflessness of three teenage boys, who spent their final moments directing their little brother away from the suffering that awaited them. I am here because of the kindness of a nameless Turkish family. I exist because Ovssana defied societal expectation and refused to persist with loveless matrimony; my great-grandmother would not allow true happiness to escape her. I exist because of the love that grew and blossomed in the darkness.

The story of my family's survival is not unique. The Armenian diaspora in its near entirety is directly descended from genocide survivors. Families are bound as one by separate tragedies that form the overarching narrative of our suffering, rubbishing the denialist arguments proposed by successive Turkish governments.

I have been researching my family's experiences with my cousin, Michelle Magarian. Her great-grandparents on her mother's side of the family, Flora and Minas Kuyumijian, lived in the town of Albāstan. They had three children together; two boys and an infant girl. The Kuyumijians were forced from their home and ordered in to separate deportation marches towards the concentration camps surrounding Deirez-Zor, in the Syrian Desert. Deportation marches became death marches. Ottoman gendarmes escorting caravans of Armenians were ferocious in their violence, bayoneting and shooting whomever they pleased. The gendarmes also allowed members of the Special Organisation, a special forces unit under the War Department, to massacre and rape deportees.

Minas was able to escape; hiding amongst the corpses that littered the Anatolian countryside, he survived the passage to Syria alone. Flora was made to undress by her tormentors. It is likely that she was raped, though she would not talk about that aspect of her ordeal. Then, on the lush banks of the Euphrates, Flora's hands and feet were bound with rope. She watched as the gendarmes drowned her children. Begging to die, she too was hurled into the water. However, Flora's instinctive desire to preserve her own life was strong and she was able to cling to the vegetation that fringed the river. A Turkish peasant rescued her, offered her clothes and then concealed her amongst the produce in the back of his cart. He personally facilitated Flora's transit to Syria. Fate then intervened; Flora and Minas were miraculously reunited in Deirez-Zor. They survived together, finally emigrating to Brazil. In Sao Paulo they had five children and lived long lives.

It is a sad fact that the Armenian genocide and the ongoing battle against the forces of denial have been decisive in shaping my identity. I can only look to the past with profound grief. The extreme violence my family endured is the foundation of our narrative. What existed before 1915 was stolen from us. If I were to return to my ancestral homeland, it would be near impossible to trace our roots; our history has been erased. I am frozen in time. I cannot move forward until our suffering is recognised. The denialist arguments proposed by successive Turkish governments are a continuation of the crime itself. Governmental denial reshapes history and demonises the victims, successfully replicating the anti-Armenian sentiment that was rife when the genocide occurred. It is a fallacy to believe that the Armenian Genocide has two legitimate histories, one for the perpetrators and one for the victims. The genocide is not an allegation, it is a fact.

Malcolm X said, 'If you stick a knife in my back nine inches and pull it out six inches, that's not progress ... The progress comes from healing the wound that the blow made. They haven't even begun to pull the knife out. They won't even admit the knife is there.'

There will be no progress without recognition.

Robert Kazandjian is an educator and writer from Edmonton, North London. His father's family's survival of genocide and his mother's unapologetic socialism shaped his thinking. His work seeks to challenge inequality and injustice in all its guises.

Why British Historians Must be De-colonised

Marcus Stow

India would like some of the British Empire's spoils back, and have made it known with a campaign to return the Koh-i-Noor diamond, worth £105m and currently set in the Queen Mother's crown. It's not of course a unique situation, as campaigns for the return of the Parthenon Marbles and other loot held in British museums gather pace. As usual, the British establishment isn't giving up without a fight, with historian Andrew Roberts positively indignant:

Those involved in this ludicrous case should recognise that the British Crown Jewels is precisely the right place for the Koh-i-Noor diamond to reside, in grateful recognition for over three centuries of British involvement in India, which led to the modernisation, development, protection, agrarian advance, linguistic unification and ultimately the democratisation of the sub-continent."

It's telling that Roberts can't even bring himself to use the word "colonialism", instead choosing "involvement", and presents India as an "undeveloped" nation prior to British rule. This is despite the fact that India was the world's largest economy for the majority of the 1,700 years before the British East India Company arrived, and was subjected to a brutal colonialism that decimated previous social systems and caused famine, disease and death. Winston Churchill himself, referring to the catastrophic Bengal famine, declared, "I hate Indians... they are a beastly people with a beastly religion." The famine was their own fault, he declared, for "breeding like rabbits."

It's not just Andrew Roberts. It's media offspring Dan Snow's misty-eyed strolls through India on the BBC, surveying filtered vistas and steam trains, presenting colonialism as a great romantic adventure for all concerned. There's Dominic Sandbrook writing in the Mail on Sunday that "Britain's empire stands out as a beacon of tolerance, decency and the rule of law". And who can forget our old friend David Starkey, of "the whites have become black" fame, who is a staunch supporter of pupils rote learning historical dates and facts but only applies critical analysis to Mary Seacole's inclusion in the National Curriculum. All of these voices are given an enormous platform and big budgets – funded by the TV licences of people of colour – on our very own BBC.

These are clever men, but clearly not clever enough to use Google, where facts about how Britain's ascendancy was funded by slavery, genocide and murder appear on page one of search results from credible sources. There is also, of course, the absence or frequent dismissal of the stories of people of colour who live in or are descended from colonised nations. Our own histories, written and oral, tell a markedly different tale, and the results of colonial brutality is literally in our genes, as demonstrated by the substantial proportion of European DNA found in black people of the African diaspora with no recent white ancestry. It's even on our birth certificates, with our original surnames being erased in favour of the people who bought our ancestors as slaves.

So why are so many of our high-profile historians, armed with first-class honours degrees, PhDs and fellowships of the Royal Historical Society, in denial about our colonial past? You might think achieving such honours would require a degree of critical thinking. Unfortunately, what we see is largely white men interpreting the dusty work of other white men, all viewed through the lens of the dominant paradigm: Britain loves to frame its former Empire and Industrial Revolution as the due consequences of Britain's unique entrepreneurship, innovation and spirit of adventure, rather than as a result of brutal colonialism and imperialism. Cotton, after all, did not grow in the fields near Manchester. This is not just a question of problematic historians: this lack of critical thinking and incorporation of the testimonies and histories of people of colour is then fed into our school curriculums and permeates our national psyche. In an admittedly unscientific poll on Twitter, I asked young people what they learned in school about colonialism. Most expressed the view that they had learned very little about its full impact on the invaded nations, with one respondent going so far as to say:

"Colonialism was completely erased when I was at school, completely and utterly. I remember I went to see 12 Years a Slave with a woman who was in my year at school. Afterwards she said, 'We may have our problems, but at least we never did anything like that'. I had to tell her that the UK was a colonial power, that we had a huge stake in the slave trade, that we had plantations. The education just wasn't there." —@thelovelymrfred

This minimising of the impact contributes to the considerable backlash for those who suggest reparations are owed for Britain's crimes. When Portia Simpson Miller, Jamaica's Prime Minister, suggested talks with David Cameron on this subject, there was a backlash on social media and from the Prime Minister himself who used the usual derailing tactic of referring to the UK's role in the abolition of slavery instead of the preceding 245 years or the ensuing involuntary servitude and instead urged Jamaica to "move on". Many made reference to Jamaica's poor record on LGBT rights, but failed to mention that entrenched homophobia, transphobia and biophobia was introduced by colonialists and missionaries in the first place. There's a consistent theme of "moving on" for events that happened "200 years ago".

Personally speaking, my mother arrived from Barbados as a British subject in the early 1960s. One of her primary reasons for leaving Barbados was that she did well academically but all the most prestigious professions, such as working at a bank or for the local telecoms company, were reserved for white people. Indeed, the telecoms company had a policy of only employing black people as chauffeurs in a country that, then as now, was only around 3% white. She left behind a cousin whose surname was Cumberbatch, a name imposed by Benedict Cumberbatch's slave-owning ancestors. His ancestors were paid today's equivalent of £3.6 million in compensation when slavery was abolished, a legacy that no doubt was re-invested and helped pay for young Benedict's private schooling. My mother and her cousin received not a penny of these legacies, and that has impacted their respective lives today.

Tales of personal experience such as this are now being told and used to challenge the dominant discourse that colonialism was largely benign. There's the high profile Rhodes Must Fall campaign at the University of Oxford whose aim is to "decolonise the space, the curriculum, and the institutional memory at, and to fight intersectional oppression within, Oxford". People of colour are using social media to campaign for the decolonisation of public holidays, such as Australia Day being mourned far more accurately as "Invasion Day", and Columbus Day in the USA being celebrated as "Indigenous People's Day". Even the phenomenon of Indigenous people telling their own stories on a rotating basis on Twitter helps people of colour to deconstruct the history we were taught at school through the lens of the coloniser. If only the British historical establishment, and by extension our media, politicians and the national curriculum, would follow suit. They could start with Google.

Marcus Stow is an IT professional who lives in Walthamstow, East London, of mixed race Bajan heritage. He's passionate about intersectionality in LGBT+ organisations and spaces, writing his thoughts at TheQueerness.com. An admitted Twitter addict, he likes to sing Whitney songs on karaoke and loves to encourage his husband to cook him gourmet meals.

Diversity is Dead, and Whiteness Killed It

Shane Thomas

People like the idea of diversity. They just don't like being around different people"

Diversity. One of those idioms that's been widely established as a good thing. Like "world peace", or "green energy". However, this appeal remains superficial, with only society's powerful having the option to implement it; an option they often refuse to enact.

Kavita Bhanot wrote about this in her essay "decolonise not diversify". The issue remains a perennial part of our news cycle, with former Prime minister David Cameron – probably after being reminded by his Chief of Staff that he needed to try and offset his statements about migrants – stating his displeasure with the lack of opportunities for people of colour in British society.

Kavita's piece was outstanding, but my quarrel isn't with the idea of diversity, it's with the defenestration of the concept. Much like American confectionery, the best thing about diversity is the packaging. While, by definition, it should be intersectionality's natural comate, diversity has become an emaciated term for talking about race (or gender that centres cis white women). Often disability, sexuality, or gender identity (among other axes of oppression) get left by the roadside.

If one were to do a straw poll, how many could explain why diversity is important? How can David Cameron – among others – espouse its benefits without justifying it beyond inchoate notions such as tolerance or British values? Diversity isn't the first thing that's been misused due to a lack of lucid understanding, and such imprecision leaves it open to manipulation by the most privileged, causing it to regress into an exercise in public relations.

Established institutions aren't saying they want diversity. At best, they're saying they won't go out of their way to prevent it, as long as they don't have to actually do anything. Often saying they value diversity means, "Look. We've got a

RME person. Now stop bothering us about it, so we can focus on important things like making money." It puts one in mind of the Langston Hughes poem, Impasse: "I could tell you/If I wanted to/What makes me/What I am/But I don't/Really want to/And you don't/Give a damn."

We shouldn't be looking only at the dearth of influential people of colour. We should be looking at the preponderance of whiteness. Rather than shielding yourself behind how many people of colour your company employs, better to scrutinise why you have so many white people.

Diversity should be a remedy, but it's often little more than a nostrum, because the dominant culture is only willing to tweak an approach that ostensibly works. It's true that many are genuinely confused and affronted when this topic is raised – "The system works, doesn't it? If it didn't, surely we would have changed it by now?"

Another favourite rejoinder is that one's identity is incidental, and talent should be the only consideration. A demand for special treatment, and an aversion to hard work is the only problem here, right?

Such myopia is as commonplace as it is asinine, and illustrates the limits of diversity when the most privileged refuse to accept complicity, such as the erroneous and unspoken assumption that diversity produces a dilution in acumen.

Variegated representation, however, isn't a corrective. Plenty who live under oppression are only concerned with evading society's malign sting, rather than trying to remove the sting altogether. As Anele Nzimande said: "Because you wanted to create robots who are compliant, who keep the machinery working, the same sort of knowledge production", while Panashe Chigumadzi added; "I call it the "add blacks and stir" model. Stir, while continuing with the same structure, same rules."

Even when we see an equitable racial mix, it can result in impedance from those in power. It promotes conflict as well as progress. And the endgame should be co-operation rather than discord. However, the source of this discord isn't online rancour, boycotting the Oscars, or #RhodesMustFall. It's white supremacy. Diversity – instead of being an agent of change – is the dominant culture's favourite remix; adding a couple of new instruments to give the false impression of a new song.

From the always essential Black Girl Dangerous site, Chanelle Adams opined; "I want a diversity that does more than change the faces that surround us from white to Brown and Black, but also demands issues that affect our communities are brought to the forefront."

A world assembled on systems of dominance and abuse didn't plan for diversity, and the disquiet can only begin to cease when those in charge accept their role in removing disparities. Thinking of hiring a woman of colour? A trans person? A disabled person? Don't. Don't hire one. Start by hiring three, at least. And race, gender, or sexuality aren't partitioned categories. They are commingled elements of our citizens, and of our country.

It's ironic how some like to talk about the disenfranchised being afraid of hard work, when getting yourself a token is incredibly lazy praxis. Yale University professor, John Dovidio said; "If you value something, it's the outcome that matters. If you want diversity in the workplace, you have to fight for it." Kyriarchy is one of society's most difficult equations to solve. And like any maths problem, you can't answer it sufficiently without showing your working.

I've written before about the positionality of Britain's people of colour as the ethnic icing on a white cake. Well, the icing isn't enough. We need to be all the ingredients: the eggs; the flour; the milk; it's not about letting us have some cake, too. It's about us being part of the cake. The focus shouldn't be on including blackness, but changing whiteness.

Shane Thomas is a columnist for Media Diversified. His work tries to bring into focus how aspects of pop culture, sport, and media functions in British society

Visible Ordinariness: The Journey Towards Protection, Acceptance and Equality for Trans People Or: Clear and Present Transgender

Suzy Wrong

Visibility for many trans people is a conundrum. Unlike our genderqueer compatriots, we often work for ideas of gender that seem to be about, above all, conformity and normality, which in turn implies a certain ordinariness and social invisibility. In early stages of our individual transitions, we are especially obsessed with achieving a gendered regularness, turning ourselves unexceptional, which for many remains a genuine priority in daily life. For others, we evolve in a different direction. We abandon the fear of notoriety, of sticking out like a sore thumb, and embrace this unique experience and, indeed, identity of being transgender.

I am a woman who does not wish to forget that I am also transgender. I value the strangeness that has been my idiosyncratic journey and honour the parallels between my understanding of the world, and those of my trans sisters and brothers. I respect our infinite differences, but recognise the one element that keeps us connected. It is a special bond that does not surmount every conflict, but our rivalries are partnered by a deep and instinctual union, like siblings of a different nature.

Some of us choose to live unassuming lives, and shun every bit of limelight that draws attention to their trans herstories. Others want to be part of this spectacular conversation that is under way in more dazzling fashion than ever before. In recent years, developed countries have suddenly become conscious of the transness that is an intrinsic part of humanity. Predictably, we have entered this discourse from a perspective of discrimination and struggles, adopting paradigms from the feminist movement, gay rights activism and racial politics. We talk about the pain and suffering, all the challenges and injustices that we face, urging our greater communities to dismantle systems of hatred that target yet another constructed notion of difference that keeps people separate and that insists on our subjugation.

November 20 of every year marks Transgender Day of Remembrance, in which we mourn all the lives lost to transphobia around the globe. As the world changes, we come to realise that a different approach to bringing trans issues to the fore is necessary, and March 31 has become a day to celebrate those who have and are in transition. International Transgender Day of Visibility is dedicated to raising awareness, and presents an opportunity for a positive focus on trans lives, in order that we may conceive of our identities beyond familiar stories of darkness. Being visible connotes not only personal coming out processes, but is also an appeal for our presence in more public domains.

Trans personalities and characters are beginning to appear on American and European screens, with Australia slowly following suit. Admittedly, we are often portrayed as objects of oddity or of tokenism, but this is a necessary stage in the short term that will lead to better modes of inclusion and representation. Transness is by and large absent from the rest of the world's media, except on occasions of tragedy and ridicule. Although difficulties are faced by trans people everywhere, we must not diminish the severity of discrimination in places where progress in this realm may not even be in its infancy, where murder based on gender and sexuality is routine and tolerated. Getting our faces on TV will not liberate all, but insisting that our voices no longer be ignored is the most important step in our current trajectory towards protection, acceptance and equality.

Like our lesbian and gay allies, coming out and using our voice is fundamentally political, and now inevitable. It is both a selfish and selfless act. It demands that our humanity and our rights be respected, and that all our potentials are given room to flourish. It also encourages others to live with authenticity and courage. It demonstrates that fear is the only real enemy, and it is the job of civilisations to work for its eradication. To be visible is to represent with resilience and honesty, without fear and shame, so that every shred of hate is turned into its opposite.

Suzy Wrong is an Australian transwoman of colour. She is Sydney's most prolific theatre reviewer

Visible Ordinariness: the journey towards protection, acceptance and equality for trans people

Your Fascination with Muslim Women's Bodies has a Long Misogynistic History

Nadia Atia

In the early hours of Wednesday 18 November 2015, Hasna Aït Boulahcen, aged 26, of Moroccan origin, was killed in an explosion in Paris. Initial news coverage of the young woman's final hours branded her 'Europe's First Suicide Bomber' and stressed a hedonistic life (see for example the Independent). In some reports, brief mentions were made of a childhood lacking in love or stability, and an adolescence devoid of religious faith. Newspapers quoted neighbours, friends and acquaintances who remembered Aït Boulahcen as a vivacious, if somewhat vulnerable, young woman, often seen in jeans and a cowgirl hat or cap before her decision to begin wearing various forms of hijab in recent months. It was later reported that Aït Boulahcen did not in fact detonate her own vest, indeed she may not have been wearing a suicide vest at all, but that the force of a blast, detonated by a male suicide bomber, scattered her body into the street. Widely circulating accounts of her spine, her head, or other parts of her body landing on the police car outside were corrected later still by reports asserting that her corpse had in fact been delivered intact to a local hospital. Unlike the initial reports, the corrections have been released quietly and have been far from front page news. At every stage, her body and its fate have been central to representations of her, and of the siege of Saint-Denis.

The astonishing level of misinformation that surrounds Aït Boulahcen's final hours, and the emphasis on her corporeality, speaks of a continued fixation on the body of Muslim woman that has its roots in orientalist and imperialist ideologies, which saw the oriental female as overtly sexualised, despite, or perhaps because of, her often hidden form. For a brief period, pictures of another Moroccan woman posing seductively in the bath were circulated in the press as images of Hasna Aït Boulahcen because she bore a 'passing resemblance'. These have now been acknowledged to be

erroneous, but their broad circulation too is a reflection
of the continued orientalist homogenisation of the Middle
Eastern female body (initial coverage was mainly by the Daily
Mail, see corrections for example from the Huffington Post).
Representations of Aït Boulahcen's life and death betray an
extraordinarily myopic view of Europe's role in shaping the
modern Middle East. While part of the appeal of Hasna Aït
Boulahcen's story was the novelty of a purported female
suicide bomber in Europe, the involvement of women in violent
attacks against European powers, and the fixation with their
bodies, is nothing new – especially not in France.

On 30 September 1956 three Algerian women Zohra
Drif, Djamila Bouhired and Samia lakhdari planted bombs in
central French-controlled Algiers. Only two of the bombs laid
by the Algerian women terrorists (to use today's parlance)
exploded in an area popular with families (Horne, A Savage
War of Peace , pp.185-186). Algiers was once one of three
Algerian provinces designated a Departement, an integral part
of France. As Benjamin Stora writes, after 1871 'Algeria had
to become a mere continuation of France on the other side
of the Mediterranean. An Algeria made up of three French
Departments would forever 'Gallicize' the territories' (Stora, p.
6.). The blasts killed three people and severely injured over fifty,
including a number of children. This bombing, like the appalling
attacks in Paris on 13 November, primarily targeted civilians
and was designed to instil fear in the established French settler
community in Algiers, known as pieds noirs.

In Algeria, the French mission civilisatrice understood
the hijab, or haik, as oppressive, and unveiling as a central
tenet of women's emancipation; ironically the result was that
the veil became a symbol of nationalist defiance, as Frantz
Fanon describes in 'Algeria Unveiled'(see Fanon, Studies
in a Dying Colonialsim and Marina Lazreg, The Eloquence
of Silence). Women who had stopped wearing it re-veiled
themselves in order to show their solidarity with the FLN,
but most emphatically to reject a version of emancipation so
closely allied with a paternalist colonial gaze. The papers have
traced Hasna Aït Boulahcen's choice of clothing from 'normal'
(the word recurs in news coverage of her last movements) or
western, attire, to a decision to begin wearing the jilbab (a
loose garment covering much of her body), and finally to her
donning of the niqab, which also covered her face. The decision
to conceal more and more of her body is directly paired with an
escalation of her involvement in the terrorist cell in the press.
Pictures of her imitating poses of premature paramilitary victory
begin to take the place of pouting teenage selfies on social

media, but in both cases Hasna Aït Boulahcen imitates familiar, unnatural poses, which appropriate her body to an exploitative patriarchal discourse, be they terrorist or glamour girl.

In a reversal of the process by which we have been led to believe that Hasna Aït Boulahcen was drawn into a terrorist cell, the women chosen for the Algerian operation needed to remove their hijabs, donning summer dresses and tinting their hair in order to 'pass' as European or 'normal' in the language of today's newspapers. This parodic enactment of colonial ideologies of women's emancipation itself seemed to strike at the very heart of French imperial life in Algeria. A number of publications reflected that Aït Boulahcen had had casual relationships, and had enjoyed alcohol and clubbing, rarely frequenting mosques and showing little or no interest in Islamic teaching or practices. Several go so far as to say that she had a 'bad reputation'. Conversely, Horne points out that the sexual allure of the Algiers bombers was central to their ability to carry out their mission and suggests that Zohra Drif eluded capture at a French checkpoint because she flirted with her interrogator (186). In both cases the sexuality of the women is crucial to representations of their militancy; in each their bodies are a grotesque spectacle to be appropriated by any manner of convenient, often misogynist, political discourses.

Though she was made famous because she represented a new threat, the elevation of Hasna Aït Boulahcen to post-mortem ignominious celebrity points us to a very old fear. The body of the veiled Muslim woman is the most visible deviation from western norms of dress, and as such it is often mistakenly read as the most obvious symbol of the failure of integration. The furore and continued morbid fascination surrounding the fate of Aït Boulahcen's body tells us far more about its symbolism as a sign of danger to European ways of life, than it does about how and why vulnerable young people are being drawn to the ideologies of violent fundamentalist movements. Nearly 60 years after the bombing in Algiers, far from representing a new threat to French society, the disturbing case of Hasna Aït Boulahcen points us to a corrosive and violating continuity in Europe's relationship with its others.

Nadia Atia is a lecturer in World Literature in the English department at Queen Mary University of London. Her work examines Britain's relationship with the Middle East, particularly Iraq/ Mesopotamia from the turn of the 20th century to the present day. Her book World War One in Mesopotamia: The British and the Ottomans in Iraq is published by IB Tauris.

Among A Race Of Others: An Overview of Western Racial Classification and Colourism

Anthony Anaxagorou

Recently, a friend asked what makes someone a 'person of colour'. For many White people and for many people of colour too, the term can seem strangely ambiguous. The ongoing refugee crisis has seen thousands of displaced people trying to enter Europe from the Middle East or East Africa, adding yet another dimension of complexity to race politics.

My friend argued that people of colour can only be Black or Asian, because Levantine and Middle Eastern people could in places pass for White, if Whiteness was simply measured by skin colour. He remarked how many Syrians had blonde hair and blue eyes; the same went for Northern Afghan, Lebanese and Palestinian groups. He mentioned how half of Turkey was geographically in Europe and its history with Greece, then claimed Cypriots consisted of either Greeks (from Greece) or Turks (from Turkey), refusing to acknowledge them as a densely heterogeneous race.

Incidentally, a case study was carried out in 2014 to test the genetic profile of 120,000 'Greek' Cypriots and 20,000 'Turkish' Cypriots. Of those examined only 23% of 'Greek' Cypriot DNA could be traced back to Greece, with people having stronger genetic links to Sicily, Iran, Turkey, Palestine, Syria, Armenia, Saudi and Syria.

As a White upper-working class heterosexual male, my friend has never had to navigate his Whiteness, along with the privileges it affords him. One of the vital components of White supremacy is keeping its beneficiaries oblivious to its authority whilst simultaneously asserting the unfounded notion of equality. White supremacy is defined as a systemic form of racism, one that believes itself to be superior in religion, intellect, culture and history when compared to those of a non-White race. To reference White supremacy is not to suggest all White people are inherently racist, but to identify the omnipresence of a damaging ideology that affects both Whites and non-Whites.

Equal opportunity forms ask people to specify their ethnicity, yet fail at being inclusive. I myself am not White, nor am I Black or Asian. I am not mixed-race either – that's if mixed-race is assumed as being half African or Asian and half European. I am Cypriot, so throughout my life I've had to tick 'other'. On paper I've always lived among a race of 'others'. In 2011 British Arabs were officially recognised in the UK census, but many forms still do not feature the option. Another misleading point here is that, aside from the Arabs of Arabia, there is no such racial group, with the association being more linguistic; however, it's become an easy point of aggregation.

I've had numerous conversations with Iranians, Cypriots, Lebanese, Turks and some North Africans who regard themselves as White. The reasons aren't necessary linked to their skin pigmentation or even their country's geography, but rather to not being Black – they have no other option but to call themselves White.

Redefining The Other

Western racial classification has always revolved around a capricious and arbitrary logic. Ancestry was once used to drive racial slavery. The one-drop rule saw that any member who had at least one person in their lineage of African descent (one drop of Black blood) would legally be considered Black. Hitler measured the noses of Jews, while other groups like the Sami of Northern Europe would be distinguished by language. Over the last thirty years that logic has shifted again to forge the current binary regard many hold for the self-identification criteria, yet it's a particular kind of Whiteness that is being imagined by those looking to see where they fit around the Black-White nexus. A key feature of the non-White/White anxiety is the psychological implication of being made to feel perennially 'other'. If within a White dominated society the very thought of being affiliated with 'Blackness' leans towards a pervasive history of oppression, social and economic disadvantage, police harassment and brutality, then the desire to run away from that narrative becomes even greater. The racial stratification in North Africa, a byproduct of Arab colonial history, also plays a huge role in drawing distinctions between Arabs (White) and Africans (Black). Those roles are then transformed when both groups enter Europe.

White Symbolism

Symbolically, the colour white has always been attributed to 'the good'. In Kenneth N. Addison's book We Hold These Truths To Be Self Evident, he demonstrates how Shakespeare was partly responsible for denoting the word 'fair', while other historians such as Nell Irvin Painter in The History Of White People suggest that references to light and dark predate the symbolism of the Judeo-Christian religions. As mentioned previously, the way Whiteness is assessed has shifted significantly over the last 500 years. When German physician J.F Blumenbach coined the term 'Caucasian' in the 19th century, he used the cephalic index and the science of anthropometry to identify the Caucasian race. Initially these taxonomic groups had little to do with skin tone and more to do with location. The Caucasian race spanned all of Europe and North Africa along with Central, Western and Southern Asia; however, as British, French and American imperialism worked its way around the globe, new classifications were put into place to define the proverbial other. Developments in biological anthropology and genealogy can also now prove how humans share 99.99% of their DNA, with only the mitochondrial element (mitochondria is a cell's chemical energy proponent) differentiating us. Still, it's easier and far more convenient to focus on our dissimilarities in the process of utilising skin colour in the political agenda of divide and rule.

The Racialisation of Islam

Since 9/11 there has been another noticeable shift. The racialisation of Islam has been inspired largely by fascistic politicians like Donald Trump and right-wing activist groups such as the EDL who, alongwith the tabloid press, refer to Muslims as if they were a race rather than a faith group consisting of many disparate races. The need to manufacture the idea of a central enemy and instil fear into Brits and Americans means these groups erroneously limit this 'race' of Muslims to those who are descended from either the Middle East or Pakistan. Never is there a mention of Southeast Asian Muslims or White European Muslims from Bosnia or Chechnya, or those who converted to Islam from other European countries.

In the hyper-racialised climate of the 21st century there is a more insidious effort to repress foreign cultural values and belief systems than ever before. Some argue xenophobia is at the helm, whilst others suggest racism. Although the two terms are used interchangeably, they do have relatively distinct meanings. Racism is more physical, with the focus being to irrationally discriminate against a person exclusively because of physical features the racist believes to reflect an inferior race. Xenophobia is more intangible, in that it is the fear of the assumed threat of a foreign group's cultural values and practices overriding its own. To say Whiteness is a complexion-based specifier is unwise. Albinism would deflate such an argument, as would a melanin study of southern Europeans. The colonial histories of the Levant and the Middle East all bear the cultural and physical hallmarks of a European, Asian and African presence, as is clearly reflected in the composition of the people. The geopolitics of a nation should also be seen as separate from a nation's peopling – Cyprus is a prime example of this.

You Look White To Me

The final argument would say that if any individual from a racial group appears White or light enough to a White person then they are, in effect, White, as the privileges reserved for White people could then be gained by them. Italian Americans along with the Irish faced various degrees of systematic persecution at the hands of the British and American establishment, and yet it was their perceived Whiteness that eventually allowed them to assimilate into society. It's also important to draw distinctions between Whiteness as a socio-political characteristic and as an aesthetic. When white-skinned Europeans tan their skin the intention is never to lose their political Whiteness, but rather to appear more desirable and vigorous. Similarly, a number of Eastern nations still associate light skin to nobility and wealth – remnants of a caste system introduced by Indo-Aryans around 1000BC.

There is no resolute answer to solve the ongoing quagmire surrounding racial classification. From what's been presented it's clear the current framework is as mercurial and flawed as the very idea of race itself. What I hope is clear is that origin exceeds complexion and to assume someone originates from a particular place simply because of how they appear is to deny all the dormant complexities of slavery, colonialism, war and persecution. We are not fixed archetypes, and until we learn to see race and colour in a more nuanced light, the need to keep explaining away our Whiteness, or our Blackness or our Otherness will endure.

Anthony Anaxagorou is British Cypriot award-winning poet, short story writer, publisher and poetry educator. He has published several volumes of poems and essays, a spoken word EP and a collection of short stories whilst having also written for theatre.

Language, Life and Love: Our Immigrant Parents

Jamal Mehmood

Yesterday I showed my mother the recitation of a poem written in praise of Urdu and its majesty. I understood much of it, but missed enough to make us both laugh. For example, I thought that when the orator was referring to the Sufi poet Amir Khusro, he was referring to the transgender community (my fellow Pakistanis will understand). We both laughed so much. It was a lovely few minutes; learning poetry from her or her mother is one of my favourite pastimes. It is never regimented, but occurs as and when it pleases – it is poetry after all. What this episode reminded me of was not only the beauty of the language, but just how much I miss of its treasures. As children our parents taught us Urdu by only responding in it, asking us to speak it or expect no response. Though it was seemingly harsh at the time, causing us to stop in our linguistic tracks, reverse, translate and proceed once more, it is something for which I am eternally grateful.

My Urdu is not perfect, but better than many of my second generation peers. It means I can communicate with family more easily, both elders here and everyone abroad, and feel closer to them. It is my foundation for understanding Punjabi and appreciating much of the tradition of Qawwali. In fact the ease I have developed in speaking our peculiar dialect of Punjabi at home has had detrimental effects on my Urdu. Woe is me! Imperfection notwithstanding, my parents have succeeded. Their children now speak their Mother tongue, and don't employ translators when visiting Pakistan. I hope that this accomplishment, when it makes itself evident, gives them a silent eruption of pride in public places that for a few fleeting moments makes the upheaval worth it. Holding on to our languages is of course not all our parents had dreamed for us before leaving, or being made to leave. I wonder if at her tender age my mother even envisaged the fate of any future children at all.

She was raised in Kemari, a coastal town in Karachi home to several ethnic groups, which might explain what her Kashmiri family was doing there and not elsewhere in the city of lights. It also explains why as well as being able to speak most dialects of Punjabi, she, her mother and sister can also speak Kutchi, which is rather useful when wanting to keep something secret. Many years ago, I visited the neighbourhood she came from. Narrow alleyways and small homes hidden in the dark is all I remember, but from conversations with family I know it is not the most prosperous part of the second city. I have been reminded by my grandfather who worked at the port that I or my uncle would have ended up as a clerk at best – if it were not for the move to England. The 'move' makes it sound like he contacted the local removal company and gave an address in Slough and jumped on a boat holding hands with his wife and children. The reality is far more complicated, and as I've mentioned before, deserves its own piece which I will write one day.

Throughout our childhood we imbibed the 'study hard now and have all you want later' mantra which finds itself in the mouths of so many immigrant parents, and it is a mantra not to be dismissed. It is partly what I want to explore. The logic of it, from the perspective of our parents, is undeniable – it makes perfect sense that we exploit state education here for material gain, as an opportunity not afforded to many of those who flew and swam here. Recently I have been thinking about this material gain as a form of reparation in the absence of reparations from the state, however that is most definitely for another essay, and probably for someone far more informed than I. This mantra almost definitely fits well into modern capitalism, and sounds eerily similar to notions of the American dream we've learnt about through pop culture. However my parents were not simply disciples of Adam Smith and Uncle Sam, ignorant of its pitfalls as a one-size-fits-all theory. Throughout my childhood, I was often told about the handicap we faced in the system, regardless of it being better than the homeland (it is only now I understand why it was better – again another story altogether). I'm sure we all remember lessons such as 'you have to work harder than them' and 'they don't want us to succeed' — it seems our parents were aware of 'they' well before DJ Khaled. So this mantra taught to us had urgency, an importance that was about survival as well as relief from a pain only our parents had seen. The reason I say all this is to say: we should understand. We should understand, literally and figuratively, where our parents are coming from. The lack of opportunity that they have seen, the poverty, the sacrifice and culture they have lived before us, all affects our relationship with them. The distance that sometimes arises between us has its roots elsewhere, and can only be tackled after both parties understand that. Our parents need to appreciate that we have no hand in creating this 'liberalised', 'modern' land we were born in and cannot escape its moulding clutches. This note is not to say there are universal and uniform fissures between our generations on every issue. There are some who understand more and some who understand less, but there are shared experiences of confusion and a lack of communication that need to be addressed. I recently answered some research questions on mental health issues within the Muslim community, and it reminds me that this is one of the problems that we might not have the terminology to discuss, in English or in Urdu. This does not mean all immigrant parents are dismissive of mental health, not at all. My own mother supported me like no other person could through my own years of trouble. It was a love and support that is inimitable, and beautiful. However it is just one of the key areas in which we seem to have a disconnect.

We have all been there, in conversations on modernity, gender issues, politics, race, career aspirations and all else under our shared sun with those who brought us to live under it. It is the lattermost I want to focus on. We are all familiar with diasporic jibes on medicine and engineering (law too, for the bourgeois amongst us) that seem to be common to most immigrant communities. It seems our penchant for hard academic work and these traditional career paths has not gone unnoticed. I remember speaking with a teacher of mine about my parents pushing me to work hard in my younger years, and the way she nodded told me she'd heard it before – and probably seen its results.

I recently had a convorsation with a friend about the need to balance our aspirations with ensuring the happiness of our parents and the dilemmas that this raises. I think it must seem somewhat alien to current (read white) popular culture with its slogans of 'chase your dreams no matter what', 'f**k what anyone thinks' and so on. The reality is far more convoluted and difficult than that, for us at least. It is far more difficult for us to pursue certain paths because we do partly understand where our parents come from – but our understanding has to grow, so that our communities do not split at the fault line of a new generation. We do understand the respectability, the security of those jobs — you'd be a fool not to. However we are also understanding more and more beyond the paradigms of our parents. The sacrifices that our parents have made have not only granted us access to traditional education but the freedom to think beyond it, to envisage a path for ourselves beyond their imagination. It may be a path that involves the kind of risk they wanted us to avoid, but recognising the possibility of it is a blessing in and of itself.

We are living in strange times. Even those seemingly secure career paths are now being laced with uncertainty. Recent events regarding junior doctor contract changes mean that many medical students are reconsidering this noble profession. Noble it may be, but our parents will understand economic security may have to come first for some. So now we come to this economy of ours that decides so much for us. The opportunities and choices that we gained through the migration of our parents do not exist in a vacuum – we also inherited the hyper-capitalism (through no fault of our parents, I might add) which now ironically whittles down options for so many. Our economy, especially to those who go through the higher education system, is now producing vague, corporate-sounding job titles for so many who had no idea what they wanted to do in the first place; it seems there is no time for exploration of that 'something else' that so many now want to do. This isn't confined to us as children of immigrants but applies to all young people. It is not a poetic stretch to suggest we are somewhat lost. It's just that for those of us with parents who dreamed that we would do things a certain way, there is yet another layer of confusion. I think the truth is we're all confused; after all, none of us have done this before.

What must never be confused is love. It is love that I want to end on.

Dear parents, we understand your wishes are only out of love. A deep love that wants us never to toil, because you know far better than us what that means. It is a love that stems from a wish that we never have to deal with those narrow streets and narrow lives again. You have broadened our outlooks and we are forever grateful. At times we seem to be looking too broadly for you to fathom; it is as if you've sent us so far beyond the mountain that there are things we can see that you can't, and we are so far that we can't see what we left behind with the naked eye. We need to sit and talk sometimes. Although we have it far easier than you did, we also face a special difficulty. The difficulty of pressure to ensure your travel was not in vain, that your upheaval was worth it, that the fruits of your labour are enjoyed all while we make you proud. We want to succeed, as everyone does, but in our own way that at times may 3com foreign to you (pun intended), and we're trying to work it out as we go. So whether we become journalists, humanitarians, artists or nothing of note, if we struggle with a malady of the mind that renders us powerless, with no time to be employed, we still love you and need you with us along the way. You are the reason we're here.

Jamal Mehmood is a 24 year old poet and writer from Kent. Winner of 'Poetry Rivals 2015'; his debut collection Little Boy Blue is due for release soon through Burning Eye Books. Along with Media Diversified, his work has been featured on the BBC and Mvslim. As well as poetry and long-form writing he is also working on some film projects in both fiction and non-fiction.

Racism is...

Shane Thomas

BBC3 recently aired a mini-season of shows focused on the topic of racism, one being Mona Chalabi's documentary, Is Britain Racist? Whatever one's thoughts of the programme, it was good to see a show which focused not just on race, but racism. Having a conversation on race is to be encouraged, but it's a largely fruitless exercise if the conversation doesn't focus on racism and its effects.

One of the best summations of racism that I've encountered came from The Nation journalist, Mychal Denzel Smith. Although not a definitive definition, it's a very useful primer.

"Ultimately, racism is a system of oppression that has disproportionately benefited those classified as "white" and regards others as second-class citizens. For a policy/thought/action/statement to be racist, it has to reinforce that second-class status."

I've said before I don't think many people actually know what racism is, and until majority consensus comprehends it, we'll never see it corrected. Yes, racism is a thing that individuals do to each other, and yes, racism is the EDL, Golden Dawn, and the n-word. But it's so much more. Such as...

Racism is how women of colour are never seen as the face of feminism, or asserting that "woman is the n*gger of the world". Racism is thinking you're doing enough because you follow Janet Mock and Laverne Cox on Twitter, but stay ignorant about the murders of transgender women of colour.

Racism is why whiteness isn't just perceived as the default, but the ideal. In the jaundiced eye of history, it's whiteness that got it right. Racism is having so much to say, yet having the powerful refuse to listen to you.

Racism is why people of colour are assumed inherently incapable, unable to do anything constructive without the guiding hand of whiteness. It's why we're seldom trusted to be the leaders of anything.

Racism is how white people have borne the financial boon of legalised marijuana. Racism is caring about state surveillance only when whites are targeted. Racism is how the particular ways mental health – such as eating disorders – affect PoC are never explored.

Racism is all those musicians who have made a fortune from playing black music, but have no regard for the culture and people – and their experiences – which created the art. Racism is assuming all black people are socially adept and loud extroverts.

Racism is thinking that your police are better just because they don't all carry guns. Racism isn't just the bullet from the police pistol. It's the unseen microaggressive cut that turns a confident spring into an anxious hobble.

Racism is getting a security job because the interviewer immediately assumes you will be "street savvy" enough to be able to spot criminals. Racism is arranging to meet a white person for a date only for them to remark, when they get dropped off by their parents, "You never told me they were black."

Racism is never being sure if that prospective partner likes you. It is being uncertain as to whether you are just an "exotic experiment" or "political statement". Racism is knowing that sex with a white person may end up as nothing more than a scandalous anecdote.

Racism hurts.

Racism is being left with nothing but bad options. Racism is PoC having to clean up a mess they didn't make. Racism is believing one is enough, especially when befriending PoC.

Racism is in the lexicon of our vocabulary, from "excited delirium" to "proper English" to thinking – as Carla Moore brilliantly unpacked – that Jamaican Patois is an antediluvian form of English. Racism is our immigration policy made flesh. Racism is thinking only certain people deserve a full life for themselves and their loved ones.

Racism is theft and the thieves lying about it. Racism is not having a home, living in a state of rootless limbo. Racism is only having value as a PoC if you can obfuscate the sins of your society through your actions. Racism is an aversion, suspicion, and erasure of anything derived from Africa.

Racism is AFRICOM, the New Alliance initiative, or the proliferation of military bases for the "United Empire of Earth".

Racism is the ultimate sin of whiteness, a sin for which amends refuse to be made and atonement refuses to be sought.

Racism is never being given a fair chance to fail. It makes being accepted as anything close to human contingent on exceptionalism. Racism is having to walk a tightrope of perfection whilst others are throwing objects at you, trying to knock you off.

Racism is in our media, discerned by the voices that are given credence. Racism is malleable, amorphous, and cunning. Islam is not a race, but make no mistake - Islamophobia is racism.

Racism is the regulations – unspoken and overt – placed on black hair, whilst any non-Anglicised name will be mocked, mangled, and detrimental to one's chances of employment. Racism is assuming that if a child is mixed-race, one of their parents must be white (normally the mother).

Racism is something that's not born, but made. It's been taught so effectively, we can all perpetrate it without thinking, like tying your shoelaces or leaving your keys in the same place when you get home. Racism is monstrous, but you don't need to be a monster to reinforce it.

Racism is a fire ignited by the right, but given oxygen by the left. It's one of many actors in society's very own Rogues Gallery, overlapping with other forms of oppression to harm the most marginalised.

Racism is the subconscious – but immediate – association of blackness with violence, instinct, sex, and danger

Racism is melanin being accepted as an indicator of a defective character. It's having the only choices open to you be humble and overlooked, or forthright and loathed.

Racism is being born with a debt that can never be sufficiently repaid. It means that PoC are forced to have an internal modulator to fade out their heritage and culture in the outside world.

As lengthy as this list is, there's so much that I missed out. Because racism is everywhere. It's the legacy of our past. It's in the construction of our present. To not accept this will make it the destination of our future.

Shane Thomas is a columnist for Media Diversified. His work tries to bring into focus how aspects of pop culture, sport, and media functions in British society.

Média Diversified. From the Lines of Dissent

Thank you

Thank you to all the writers and editors who have contributed to Media Diversified both past and present. Without their generosity and hard work this book would not exist.